"This volume is like a breath of fresh air! Within minutes of starting to read I realised why it was so vital for me to delve into this extremely essential reading, not only enhance my happiness, but to understand the pathway to balance my own ecology. Each chapter is deserving of merit as a stand alone concept. This book is an extremely useful tool in allowing us to tell our own story and to understand ourselves. Reading it is certainly helping me reconnect with the soul inside myself.

Michael Bagraim MP
Member of Parliament, South Africa

"What makes this book truly captivating is Laurence's remarkable breadth of knowledge, as well as his spiritual attunement. He draws on literature, film, music and history—often sharing little-known facts and hidden gems that bring freshness to familiar themes. These wide-ranging references make the book as fascinating, as it is nourishing, offering not only wisdom but also a sense of discovery with every page. I found myself using this book as a daily meditation practice, because the depth of Laurence's work invites pause and contemplation. At a time when many of us crave deeper meaning, but are swept up in immediacy and disconnection, this book is a gentle antidote. It nurtures both curiosity and a spirit of exploration. That, after all, is what living is about. Enjoy it!"

Rev Berry Behr
Interfaith Ambassador

LIVING IN TUNE WITH YOUR SOUL

LAURENCE GAWRONSKY

First Edition published by Laurence Gawronsky in 2025

Address 33 Willow Road Newlands 7700 South Africa.
E-mail: LGawronsky@outlook.com
If you wish to correspond with the author, use this e-mail.

Editing: Cathy Eden
Typesetting and layout: Elsabe Gelderblom, Farmdesign.co.za
Cover Design: Nick Jooste of NicDesign
Legal Advisor on Copyright: Adams and Adams Attorneys.

Every effort has been made to acknowledge all quotes and references. If a
reference has been omitted by error, or if there is a factual mistake,
please contact the author to amend any mistake for inclusion in the digital
edition or reprints.

Contents

Introduction

In this book I consider how to live in a more harmonious way. Living with an enlightened perspective energizes the soul and makes life meaningful. Rather than a life dominated by external forces, it is moving toward the more expansive experience of living in tune with our soul.

When writing I considered themes that were current at the time. I hope to convey insight while making references to politics, climate change, Covid-19, theatre, music and issues in the media. I view this wide range of interests from my core theme of having an enlightened life while living in the world the way it is.

I welcome you on this journey based on a concern for the truth and the expression of love leading to a state of inner harmony and accord.

1

Rewriting Our Story

In late 2019, I saw a 'one woman' show by Zolani Mahola at the Baxter Theater in Cape Town. She was the former lead singer of the famous Afro-fusion group "Freshly Ground". Freshly Ground, along with Columbian singer Shakira, played the official song of the 2010 FIFA World Cup titled "Waka Waka (This Time for Africa).[1] They performed the song to a TV audience of over 700 million viewers from around the world during the closing ceremonies of the FIFA World Cup.[2]

In her solo show, Zolani shared her life story in a theatrical presentation with singing, acting and storytelling. The presentation was inspiring and entertaining. She spoke about her life, starting with her childhood, to becoming a rock star and traveling across the world. She then lived with the consequences of that success, including losing her identity through alcohol abuse, despite the fame she achieved. Although she did not say it this way, what she was describing was living out of tune with her soul. By making some changes and venturing into a career as a solo artist, she rediscovered her authenticity. The audience watching Zolani was participating in the experience together with her, and it was uplifting.

Sometimes people share about their life, but it's not constructive in that they are rehashing the unhappiness that they have rehearsed many times in their mind. Over and over again they repeat the issues they are unhappy about. They may have a friend who will sympathize and take their side, as they tell the story of how unhappy they are. Rather than live in a way that perpetuates an unhappy state, the alternative is to find a way to make changes, to turn in another direction and then share the story of one's life in a way that uplifts and indicates a change, as Zolani did.

If the story of your life is full of unhappiness, then consider that you need to rewrite your story. That is to re-craft the story of our lives by going in a different direction.

The night before I went to Zolani's presentation, I attended an event at the Barnyard Theater, Cape Town, where there was a "tribute band" performing "golden oldie" rock songs They played and sang popular hits from the 70's, 80's and 90's, with backup dancers. They were experienced musicians and were able to reproduce these songs, but what they played was not exciting, unique or original.

When we spiritually come alive, we are not just repeating old concepts and ideas, relying on rehashed quotes and well-worn cliché's, truisms that say nothing that is new or interesting. Rather than pretending or projecting an image to try to impress, we do the work to rewrite our story. It is an expression of an original perspective that comes from living in a way that is authentic and fresh. Then we can share in a way that is "freshly ground"

2

The Ecology of Sharing

Ecology is defined in the Collins Dictionary as 'the study of the relationships between plants, animals, people, and their environment, and the balances between these relationships'.[3] Through scientific research in ecology, it is evident how these relationships are mutually beneficial. At the core of nature is sharing, with no entity isolated to itself. To be isolated with only an extractive and self-serving interest is a lonely and vulnerable existence. This is because the supporting systems and networks break down.

Living an inspired life can't be done separate from everybody else. The universe works through interchange and reciprocation. The more we study ecology, the more we discover reciprocal activity in nature. What matters is how we engage together, so that there is a sharing that is generative in what we say, what we do and in invisible ways as well. The increase in the use of media platforms can be seen as an extension of the 'ecology of sharing'. When sharing at the physical level we are also sharing in a way that is invisible as well. It is essential to connect and share in a constructive way that benefits all. In 2019, I attended a talk by Dr Walter Willies at The Eight O'clock Club in Rondebosch Cape Town.[4] Dr Willies is a retired academic from North-West University in South Africa. In his talk, he spoke about sharing and noted that, "when you write down your story, it becomes real." When we authentically share through writing, it clarifies our thinking.

We also have to be careful not to use writing in a destructive way using content that is unsubstantiated, opinionated, dishonest, negative or nasty. I find writing is an opportunity express myself, connect with people and move towards greater clarity of thought. When I write, sometimes I find it difficult to select the right words so as to find a way to express that is in tune with my soul.

To be creative, I have to apply my mind constructively, especially when replying to an email or engaging on social media. I have to take into account that what I say may be misconstrued or misunderstood. It may not be received in the way it was intended. The reader may find what I say patronizing and may spread it around it to create controversy.

In his talk, Dr Walter Willies asked us to consider that, "we do not know what our story is until we hear ourselves telling it." It takes some courage to tell one's story in an authentic way. When we express what we are thinking, rather than keep our thoughts bottled up, it may create an opening to consider an alternative view. Authentically telling one's story in a safe space, without a fixed view or agenda, creates fresh perspective. When we engage in dialogue with an open mind, it releases fixed ways of thinking and creates new insights.

We will remain locked in an old limiting story if we are just complaining about what is wrong and how others should change, without having an honest look at ourselves. The key is to not become self-righteous and to keep an open mind. It is important in expressing one's truth to be honest and open, and also to recognise what the situation is. The tone of what we express, back of what we say, makes a difference to the outcome.

3

The Immortality Project

When I was a student at the University of Cape Town, there was a small art gallery three houses down the road from where I lived. It was the former house of an artist Irma Stern, that had been opened to the public a few years after she died. I regularly walked past the gallery, but never went in.

Forty years later I was invited to an event at the gallery and was amazed at the quality of the colorful expressionist artwork. On entering the gallery, I found the experience vibrant and inspiring. Irma Stern's art was initially unappreciated in South Africa, where critics derided her early exhibitions.[5] The art is much more valuable now than when she was alive.

She had been an eccentric figure around Cape Town and yet she produced extraordinary pieces of art, which now fetch over a million dollars at auctions. I had missed out seeing her work, day after day, when I walked past the gallery without going in. There may be opportunities that we just walk past, if we don't see the possibility of opening ourselves up to something different, fresh and new.

Most artists are forgotten, and their work is of little value, yet there are also iconic artists like Stern whose work has gained in value over time. This reminded me of the academic Ernest Becker who wrote that some people have an 'Immortality Project'[6] to leave a legacy after they die. Artists can leave a legacy that continues on through the art they create.

There are many ways one can leave behind a lasting legacy. Through having a family, one can leave a legacy in that one's children continue to live after one has died. Yet I know very little about my grandfathers who had died before I was born, and even less about my great-grandfathers. So just having a family may not mean that you get to be remembered. Most people when they die, are forgotten after two generations, as they don't leave a lasting legacy. But the aim of immortality project is to know that one's life has been worthwhile. That instead of living a meaningless existence surviving from day to day, one's life is filled with meaning and worth.

A few individuals have a breakthrough in consciousness, and they are remembered for that because the way they thought changed the collective consciousness. The Bible for example, catalogs individuals who left their mark on history. This includes Abraham, Moses, The Prophets and Jesus, who had an experience of living in tune with their soul, and whose teachings have lasted for thousands of years. They left behind an 'Immortality Project' that has transformed consciousness. There are also people in the sciences such as Galileo, Pasteur, Newton, and Einstein or in the social sciences such as Freud, Jung or Marx that also left behind an 'Immortality Project' in that their work is revered long after they have passed. In creating their 'Immortality Project' they broke with the old tribal, academic or cultural patterns of thinking and belief. They brought something new in the way they thought. But they also may have encountered some resistance to what they had to offer.

It isn't easy for an individual to have a breakthrough, as many new ideas aren't readily accepted. Even in the field of science where new ideas are mathematically proven, some of the breakthroughs were well received when initially proposed, while others were criticized and challenged as they upset the status quo. There will always be people still loyal to the old way of thinking or with a vested interest in what they believe. It takes some courage to break with the prevailing ways of thinking and express it, write it down or create it.

4

Soulmates

Congressman John Lewis once said: "Never give up, never get lost in a sea of despair, never become bitter, never hate, because hate is too much a burden to bear."[7] Lewis was speaking about the political struggle for rights and justice, but we can also apply his words to our personal lives.

We all deal with people we don't agree with or who provoke anger. At times we may feel that we want to give up. It is a normal human emotion to feel overwhelmed by circumstances, yet we can find the strength to carry on and not slip into a sea of despair or bitterness. We are here to discover an alternative; to rise above the toxic state and be enlightened by a true expression of our inner soul.

Wikipedia says this about the meaning of the word 'soul': "the Hebrew word נֶפֶשׁ, *nephesh*, although translated as 'soul' in some older English Bibles, actually has a meaning closer to 'living being'.[8] So we could use the words 'soul' and 'living being' interchangeably. Carl Schultz wrote that the Hebrew word *nephesh* appears 755 times in the Old Testament.[9] In the Bible, 'soul' is an important recurring spiritual theme that can be understood and experienced.

When the word *nephesh* was translated into English, it was found that there were more words that could describe its meaning, depending on the context in which it was used. Scholars searched the Bible to see how this word was translated as there is a greater degree of subtlety in the English language. Schultz says, "The King James Version uses 42 different English terms to translate the word *nephesh*. The two most common renderings are 'soul' (428 times) and 'life' (117 times)."[10]

I am not just looking at the lexicography of these words; I am considering what it means to have the experience of 'soul' amplified in my life. To do so I have to reconnect with the Soul inside myself.

As an individual soul or living being we are connected to all 'living being' for as long as we are alive. We should not think of ourselves as isolated souls detached from 'living being'. In a mentally detached state people feel lost and experience isolation and despair. But when they align with their inner soul they can thrive and feel spiritually connected to all life and the burdens of hopelessness, anger and hate either dissipate or become diminished.

In our personal lives we see people who are erratic, and the cause of this behaviour is that at their core they have lost their connection with their soul. We need to be in tune with our soul rather than be discordant and filled with anxiety, worry or resentment. If we have lost our sense of balance anchored in a soul-based identity, it is easy to slip into an erratic state

But the key is to know that at the soul level we can love and are loved, no matter what happens in our lives.

Some people think that their life's purpose is to find their soulmate. A soulmate is often described as someone with whom one shares unconditional love with mutual respect through a connection of mind and heart. But we can all be soulmates to each other by sharing a finer quality of friendship at a soul level. Soulmates are not necessarily confined to the context of a romantic relationship. There is a popular idea that once we find our soulmate we will live happily ever after, but immaturity, selfishness and inadequacies inevitably resurface. If we haven't found the soul within ourselves, it is more difficult to sustain a soul connection with another person. To come into alignment with our own soul means we are more able to express kindness and understanding towards other people.

When one is in tune at the soul level, one has the inherent maturity to maintain a soulmate friendship with another person. When we are in touch with our soul it makes us feel more vibrationally in tune and resonant at the core of ourselves. This is beyond likes and dislikes, opinions or justifications. Rather, we see and understand the value of being connected to others, 'soul to soul'.

When we are in tune with our 'soul', we are resonant with all 'living being'. As we are aligned with our soul it uplifts us and sends out a positive energy to other people who will sense that it is safe to have a soul connection with us. Then we lay a foundation for sustaining genuine and honest relationships with others who are attuned to their 'soul' so as to be genuine soulmates together. As we develop our ability to be an enlightened soul, our capacity to have a soul connection with others increases.

5

Survival of the Friendly

Brian Hare of Duke University and his wife, Vanessa Woods, who is a scientist and researcher, have written a book called *Survival of the Friendliest*.[11] It is a variation on the evolutionary theme, 'survival of the fittest' from *On the Origin of Species* by British naturalist Charles Darwin.[12]

The idea of survival of the fittest is a way of describing the mechanism of natural selection and is not to be confused with physical strength, tactical brilliance or aggression. In watching TV this week, I noticed how many of the stories had the hero using all of these tactics! Yet often, using physical strength and aggression is not the best strategy to survive or thrive. Even in evolutionary theory, by 'fittest' Darwin meant 'better adapted to the environment.'

When we watch movies, they often have themes that are violent and aggressive rather than friendly and nurturing. To thrive, we need to move away from that way of thinking, which comes from being alienated, isolated and thereby just surviving, rather than giving and receiving in a generative way.

The theme of the book by Hare and Wood is that the quality that made us 'fit', from the perspective of evolution, was friendliness. That is, an ability to share, coordinate and communicate with others. The interchange of ideas is also the basis of many of the cultural and technological marvels achieved in human history, where scientists and academics have worked together and co-operated to have a breakthrough. Co-ordinating, having conversations and creating together allows humanity not only to survive, but also to thrive and grow beyond a pattern of survival.

Just surviving is living a difficult life whereas the opportunity is available to thrive at a mental and spiritual level. This implies not acting as a lone soldier struggling all by ourselves against all odds. Instead, we thrive through finding ways to have conversations, be open and honest, encourage growth and have an ability to create a safe place through friendliness. There may be times where we have to navigate our way carefully in a conversation to maintain friendship and not antagonize a friend or family member. We will find that the network in which we live will thrive as we cultivate friendliness.

The years leading up to 2020 was a time of improved in global cooperation and trade, but unfortunately there were also underlying political forces splitting the world apart. Countries around the world had benefited by the global cooperation which reduced prices and created employment and wealth. As nations become more friendly, they thrive, whereas when they get bogged down in conflict and war, including trade wars, the wealth and wellbeing of their citizens diminishes.

Moving beyond surviving into thriving takes learning how to reciprocate. It is not just, *What can I get for myself? How can I benefit, manipulate, dominate, or justify to my advantage?* The alternative is considering an energetic that we can share together in the spirit of friendship, by relating in a way that is generative, cooperative and friendly.

There are people who are depletive, because their only aim is to get for themselves. They don't see that they can co-operate, or that by helping other people to thrive they indirectly benefit as well. When we bring human goodness into the frame in which we live, we change the pattern not only for ourselves but for the community in which we live. As other people thrive, so do we.

6

A Node of Light

In Biblical times, for a period of almost four centuries, the Judean priesthood used the Temple in Jerusalem to perform rituals, preach and the tell stories about the past. The preaching was centralized in the Temple, with the knowledge held by the priesthood. A wide range of stories and sacred texts passed down from generation to generation formed the basis of their oral teachings.

When the temple in Jerusalem was destroyed by the Babylonian King Nebuchadnezzar, after the siege of Jerusalem, the Israelites from the southern Kingdom of Judea went into exile in Babylon around 587 BCE.[13] They took their knowledge with them, but there was a concern that without a Temple and a priesthood, it would be forgotten.

The Judean exiles learned the skill of writing down a narrative from the Babylonians. They created the Torah in a more structured way, which became the first five chapters of what we know as the Bible. The letters of the Hebrew alphabet and the structure of the language were influenced by the Babylonian texts when they were written down.

The Old Testament of the Bible as we know it was redacted, edited and transcribed in Babylon during the exile. The stories and teachings were transcribed in such a way that they could be used anywhere, far away from the Temple in Jerusalem, without requiring a centralised priesthood. It is remarkable how the stories were preserved and then written into what became the Bible. The stories were filled with truth, wisdom and understanding and they included tales about history, battles and prophecies.

In the original version of the Bible, the word 'Elohim' in the Hebrew text was translated into the word 'God' in the English version. What is interesting to note is that 'Elohim' is plural even though 'God' is seen as one God by the Jewish people.[14] Using modern thinking, Elohim can be seen as one network where there are many nodes, rather than as an entity with human characteristics. God is seen as one network that is connected together, rather than an individual, and in this network, some nodes shine brighter than others.

As we discover the truth and express life, we can be a node of light, shining in darkness as part of the network of light. Using network thinking, we can all be individual nodes in a spiritual network. We are part of the spiritual network to the degree that we take care of our own individual spiritual connection. Every living thing that embodies Being, is connected to all Being.

In some way this is similar, but obviously technically different, to the way computers and cell phones are connected to the 'one internet' with each connection as a node that has access to the entire network. It can be said that we are connected in spirit as part of a network of God.

We may think we are just a little drop in the ocean of consciousness and that our consciousness doesn't matter. But it does, because as one node in the collective consciousness is freed up to be a brighter point of light, it allows the whole network to be more enlightened to some small degree.

We are all individual nodes inside a collective consciousness and as one light goes on in just one node, it makes a difference to all the other nodes, creating an opportunity for greater transmission across the spiritual network. If we have a flat TV screen and a few diodes are not working, there will be a black spot. Likewise, some individuals are dark spots in the picture of humanity.

We can then live as a node of light in the field of

consciousness. We may underestimate ourselves as a point of light, but it makes a difference. The more points of light, the brighter the network. When we are in tune with our soul we can then live as a node of light in the field of consciousness.

7

Being and Becoming

The idea that we are human beings has been around a long time. The use of the word *'being'* dates back to the writings of Plato and Aristotle[15] and is also mentioned in Psalms and in Proverbs in the Bible.[16] There is a citation dated 1666 in the On-line Etymology Dictionary on the use of the words 'human being' describing a mortal human who also has an invisible spiritual quality of *being*.[17] The term 'human being' has been in the English language for over 350 years. It is a recognition that we are not just human, but also a *being*.

Gravity is invisible and yet it affects everything on earth as it keeps us on the planet and the planet in orbit around the sun. There is also an invisible realm of *being* that affects the quality of our lives. At this stage, unlike gravity there are no mathematics to prove that at the core of ourselves, we are *beings*.

Each religion or belief describes God or spirit differently. But regardless of what you believe or how you name your spiritual source, what matters is whether at a core level you are taking care of your experience of *being* and expressing that in your life. As we align with *being*, we are connected to and enlivened by the source of life throughout the universe. When we are aligned with *being*, we live in tune with our soul, and have a greater experience of aliveness. This applies no matter what the belief or religion is. If, as a human, we are not in harmony with *being* we will experience alienation, disempowerment and emptiness.

Instead of seeing ourselves as humans having beliefs, we can see ourselves as *beings* having a human experience. When Plato and Aristotle considered the "Metaphysics of Being and Becoming" they saw *being* as part of our essential nature that does not change. Conversely, *becoming* was seen as the way the natural world and our lives are always changing. So, we can see ourselves as a *being* that is *becoming*. As we come to a greater sense of knowing the *being* at the core of ourselves, we find a resonant inner state of harmony that transcends the human state.

In the process of *becoming*, we may find that the continuity of our lives gets disrupted and changes. There are many causes of this change, including failed relationships, illness, loss of employment, the collapse of a project, a change in finances or an injury. At that time, the way our lives have been constructed comes to an end. This change in circumstances then forces us to redirect the direction and narrative of our lives.

Then we may find that we have to reinvent ourselves as a different person. We do that by opening up to new experience. This may include an openness to spiritual experience and philosophic understanding. When that happens, it is useful to have an anchor in invisible *being*, while one is *becoming* something else.

Teilhard de Chardin said, *"We are not human beings having a spiritual experience, but spiritual beings having a human experience."*[18] That is a journey to come to a greater sense of knowing *being* at the core of ourselves. It is not just a journey in the external world such as a journey around the earth, but a journey into a resonant inner state of harmony, that transcends the usual human experience.

Even if our outer circumstances change, our alignment in *being* can still be consistent. But most people live their lives blindsided from the perspective of *being* in that they don't take care of themselves as a living *being* and live in a state of discord. An alignment with our inner sense of *being* provides continuity.

If we don't look after our *being* nature, there will an inner void as there is something at the core of ourselves, that is dissipated. There will be people who try to undermine us or suck up the energy of the people around them to boost their ego, while they undermine the lives of others. But it is important to not let our energy be dissipated in that way.

Through the expression of *being* we will find that we can cope with whatever is changing, and we become more able to adapt as we continue in our *becoming*. When our inner core is connected with the invisible quality of resonant harmonious energy, which is another way of describing '*being*', we feel more alive. This is not something we can measure and evaluate in a tangible way, but we know it when we experience it and live in the transcendent state.

8

Spiritual Beings Having a Human Experience

As mentioned in the previous chapter, Pierre Teilhard de Chardin said: *"We are not human beings having a spiritual experience; we are spiritual beings having a human experience."*[19] Having this perspective we will be less inclined to take events personally, as it provides a foundation that helps us deal with changes creatively. When we think we've got it all sorted out, it's easy to act in a way that is arrogant and opinionated. Identifying as a "spiritual being having a human experience" we learn humility when facing difficulty.

There will be unexpected events that seem threatening, which may include:

- Military service, military conflict or regime change,
- Academic failure or project disappointments,
- Financial fraud, loss or theft,

- Fires, storms, floods and droughts,
- Motor vehicle accidents,
- Unrest, riots and strikes,
- Unemployment/retrenchment,
- A business venture going insolvent,
- The passing of parents (or spouse/life partner),
- Financial reversals and crashes,
- Serious illness (personally or to a close member of family).

At some stage in my life, I have experienced most of these events. I was able to consider philosophically that these events are part of the human experience that most people have. At the time, I was able to hold my spiritual identity as a "spiritual being having a human experience" come back in tune with my soul, make changes, and move on.

By living a philosophically inspired life, despite the difficulties and setbacks, I have an inner knowing that all is well. I focused on living in the present moment, maintaining my orientation, free from regret about the past or anxiety about the future. I continued doing what was possible to take the next step forward in a way that is honorable, trustworthy and caring.

How we act when on a downward trajectory has an impact when the direction turns upward again. When facing adversity, if the person collapses in a heap or feels overwhelmed by outer forces or thinks that it's unfair, they won't be in position to go with the flow when the tide turns. We need to understand that our inner experience makes a difference in maintaining our identity in a turbulent world. We can undermine ourselves if we do not hold steady and see what is possible.

No matter how difficult life is, we always have an opportunity in the present moment to lay a foundation for future growth.

9

Authentic Relationships

The philosopher Thomas Paine wrote pamphlets that inspired the American Revolution.[20] He came from England where he has had a difficult life, including experiencing bankruptcy before moving to America. He once said, "He who dares not to offend cannot be honest."[21]

While honesty carries the risk of offending some people, the opposite extreme was demonstrated by President Donald Trump, who made what were regarded by his opponents as offensive comments on social media. President Trump had opponents who mocked, criticized, and vilified him for speaking his mind, sometimes unfairly so. Yet he also had many loyal supporters who were pleased that he did not filter his speech.

I am not suggesting that there is an advantage to acting in a way that is perpetually offensive. Nor am I suggesting that writing or speaking in a way that is politically incorrect, implies authenticity. Rather, I am considering having greater experience of the expression of truth in an authentic way.

Many countries suffer from leadership that is: inauthentic, make false promises, have a lack of integrity or do not act in the best interests of the nation. During the first two weeks of December 2019 there were protests on the streets of Hong Kong, Bangkok, London, Mumbai, Beirut, Iran, the DRC, Chile and across France, as well as service delivery protests in South Africa. Economic and political concerns drove the protests, and the issues in each country were different. The people protesting around the world were frustrated because they felt they were politically and economically disconnected and alienated. This not only applies in the political and economic spheres, but in other areas of our lives as well.

There are many who feel disconnected and alienated at the core of themselves. It is better to resolve these feelings through engagement and discussion, rather than protest. It does not get resolved by making disparaging comments. As we engage with an open mind, we can discover what the truth is.

Through dialogue and an openness to learn, we will feel more connected. Authentic relationships are not always easy. They require maturity and openness as well as compassion and understanding. It is much easier to pretend and to have 'politically correct' relationships in which we act as if everything is 'okay', rather than having genuine interaction.

When we have an authentic conversation about our life, we may find ourselves having to go into areas that are uncomfortable. We may also have our own political correctness questioned and be called to task. If one is out of tune or feeling alienated, it requires honesty to bring oneself back to being resonant with the core of truth within oneself.

When we take care of the atmosphere in which we live, and are living in tune with our soul, there is an experience of wellbeing. Having a consciousness that is inspired by our alignment with the truth, brings perspective into our current circumstances. We can go into situations that are challenging and know that we are not isolated and powerless. When aligned with the truth, we feel connected in a way that is empowering. We may still have to overcome resistance, but will have more real and rewarding relationships.

10

War or Peace

At the time of writing this chapter there were numerous wars around the world, some not receiving much attention. Technology had also significantly changed the way that war is conducted. By the end of 2019, which was regarded as a peaceful time, the United States of America, as the global superpower, was involved in at least seven different types of war. These wars ranged from the physical to the technological, all of which have had unintended consequences.

The wars were:

- The War on Terror (in Middle East and Africa)
- The Cold War (sanctions on Russia and Iran)
- The War on Drugs (drug abuse and gangs)
- The Climate War (fighting climate change)
- Trade and Currency Wars (tariffs and limiting access to finance)
- Info Wars (propaganda via news and social media)

- Cyber Wars (computer viruses, ransom-ware and spy-ware).

These wars continued with no clear-cut resolution or understanding of the effect they have on people, politics, economics or the environment. In every one of these wars there have been unanticipated outcomes for the affected populations. There were no easy solutions or outright victors to these wars. Documents released by the Washington Post in 2019 included one written in 2015 where a commander in Afghanistan Lieutenant General Douglas Lute said, "What are we trying to do here? We didn't have the foggiest notion of what we were undertaking." [22]This he said after 14 years of fighting! He then went on to say that they weren't even clear who the enemy was. This was also happening in other wars and conflicts that perpetuate without an end in sight.

In every war there are winners and losers, which can also change over time, when one side or the other gains the advantage. Wars often morph in ways that were not envisioned or intended. The conflict on the ground often does not match the lofty rhetoric or beliefs. In all these wars that the USA was involved in, it was not clear what the effects will be on the American people or the global economy in the long run.

Regarding Climate War, the climate doesn't care

about political boundaries, ideology, or economic goals. The heat wave in Australia during December 2019 had air temperatures averaging over 40° C, which caused more than 100 massive fires.[23] Australians unexpectedly found themselves on the front line of the Climate War, when the common perception was that Australia was too isolated to be facing much threat. We are part of a global, interconnected world moving in unexpected ways, and must cope with unforeseen changes.

There will be situations that we find ourselves in that are not governed by a clear vision of possible consequences. It may not be possible to stop the war between countries, or any of the other forms of war, but it is always possible to address the state of conflict in ourselves. To meet the challenges that come to us in a creative way that brings clarity and perspective, even when encountering aggression or threat.

11

Awareness Leads to Change

In December 2019 there was a story in the news media about a small town in Northern Russia. More than 50 polar bears had migrated a few kilometers and invaded a town on the Novaya Zemlya Archipelago,[24] due to the loss of habitat caused by climate change. That may not seem life threatening as some have a memory of a Coca-Cola ad, with a cartoon of a happy polar bear wearing a red scarf drinking a bottle of Coke.[25] However, polar bears have been known to hunt and kill humans, so having so many in town is a very dangerous situation!

At the same time, there was the 2019 United Nations Framework Convention on Climate Change in Madrid.[26] There were half a million people out on the street protesting outside the Summit, urging the nations of the world to take climate change seriously. Greta Thunberg, a well-known young climate activist, arrived in Madrid,[27] having previously spoken to the

UN Assembly in New York, saying: "People are suffering. People are dying. Entire ecosystems are collapsing". In her remarks, Thunberg accused politicians of pretending that the world's dire climate problems can be solved with technical solutions. But she said that they continued as if it was, "business as usual."[28]

Based on archaeological records, there has been climate change throughout history. Milankovitch cycles are a framework for understanding long-term changes in the Earth's climate, including the beginning and end of Ice Ages over the Earth's long history.[29]

According to biblical records, there were floods and famine, which we can assume was caused by climate change. At the time the Bible was written they did not use the term 'climate change' and assumed that that significant changes in climate, including drought and floods, was retribution for disobeying God.

Through research using meteorological data, climatologists have a better understanding of these changes. Researchers have hypothesized the role that human beings are playing in the acceleration of climate trends. Yet, global corporations and government institutions are finding it difficult to direct investment away from fossil fuels.

There is a world view that we are increasingly encountering difficult times. With an increase in floods, fires, hurricanes, heat waves and drought some predict that ongoing climate change places civilization under threat of collapse. For the first time, we are at least globally aware that the climate is changing, which is a positive step. Based on the information available, we can change. Having an awareness of what is causing the changes opens a door for change, as we are then no longer blaming God. In the 21st century we are living in an era where can take some responsibility to make intelligent changes.

There is now an awareness of many natural and scientific phenomena that were not previously understood. There have already been many discoveries that humans have made for the betterment of humankind. This includes meteorology, the invisible radio wave spectrum and the micro world of germs and viruses. Interventions such as the application of vaccines, sterilization and cleanliness have prevented disease and saved many millions of lives. According to Johan Norberg "it is largely unknown fact that humanity is now healthier, happier, cleaner, cleverer, freer and more peaceful than ever before".[30]

Awareness of changes in the outer world must be matched with an inner understanding, so that we can receive this information in an intelligent way. Just knowing about the potential of floods, fires, hurricanes, drought, or economic collapse isn't enough if we are not collectively prepared to understand what is happening and make changes.

Likewise, when we take care of our inner climate, how we interpret what we think and how we feel, we will have the clarity to adjust to or accept the changes as they happen. We can then find creative ways to deal with whatever circumstances we are in with greater perspective and understanding, and do something about it.

12

An Interesting Conversation.

On 4th November 2019, there was an interview between controversial radio host, Howard Stern and comedian Trevor Noah, who at the time was hosting "The Daily Show" a late night TV program. In the interview, Noah recalled his first appearance before a large audience when he was selected as the opening act for the well-established comedian, Dave Chappelle.

At that time Noah asked, "What am I even doing here?" Chappelle answered that Noah was there not just because he was funny but because he was interesting. Chappelle said, "Anyone can be funny, but they may not be interesting."[31] It was Noah's range of life experience that made him relatable and interesting. Comedian Trevor Noah was able to engage in interesting dialogue, and he did so on his TV show.

Any conversation that includes perspective based on life experience is more interesting than a catalog of opinions regarding the issues and struggles that the individual is facing. They may be struggling with victimhood, recounting how they have suffered or been slighted. If the conversation has no interest in developing insight, or understanding of how to adapt to achieve to a better outcome, it is less interesting. That is a conversation that is not restricted to complaint or only focusing on constraints and limitations. Rather it is a conversation that is filled with curiosity and consideration of possibilities. Comedian Trevor Noah was able to engage in interesting dialogue, and he did so on his TV show.

It is not that we judge the range of conversation or think less of people who have a narrow range. Back of the conversation, the questions are:

- Is there any understanding of what is happening?
- Is there an interest in the larger world?
- Is there any inquiry beyond the most immediate circumstances and their effects?
- Is there any perspective and insight?

When talking to somebody who has a narrow view, there is only so far that the conversation can go before it shuts down, either through an emotional reaction or lack of depth. Range broadens when there is a willingness to listen and an openness for personal growth. That then becomes a more enlightened and deeper conversation.

One of the core factors in expanding the range of conversation is whether there is maturity in the individuals concerned. If so, the conversation can go further because there's perspective and understanding in the way the content of the conversation is received by each party. It also helps if individuals have a lightness of being, so that humor may be included to highlight how funny and bizarre some situations are. Then life experience can be shared in a relaxed, insightful and encouraging way.

The underlying consideration behind any conversation is whether an individual has a philosophy that guides their life. Is there philosophic inquiry that is broad and infinite? If people have a philosophy, but their beliefs are fixed and narrow, they will lack insight and take a hard-line approach and be inflexible. If they are open, they can go beyond the immediate circumstance to discover new perspectives. Is there an openness to having an experience of transcendence, inspired by spiritual understanding? When such openness is present, the range of conversation is more expansive.

It is not enough to have an abstract philosophy that is theoretical, but never applied. I have met people who have an impersonal philosophy that they have read, learned and studied, which has not been integrated into their life. They do not have a philosophy in the first person; it's a philosophy in the third person and not something that they personally experience day- to-day. Personalizing one's philosophy requires questioning and testing, to find how that philosophy is applied in real life.

There will be times when one fails to live up to high ideals and it requires honesty when that occurs. It is important to acknowledge when something should have been said or done differently, or that one's life has gone in the wrong direction. Recognizing mistakes and failure, will lead to learning and growth, so that the underlying philosophy is congruent with life experience and lessons learned. It is not just about being right or trying to impress. Rather, the philosophy is used as a guiding light. Through an openness to new perspectives, understanding and wisdom, we become relatable and interesting.

13

Connected

I was in a conversation using the Zoom App for an internet video call with people located on three continents. I was in the southern hemisphere, in Cape Town, and many of the participants were in North America and Europe. Yet we participated in one conversation using the internet. We were connected in conversation as if space and time did not matter. For the first time in history, we can have multi-station, face- to-face conversations, regardless of where we are in the world. Dial-up telephones had been around for 100 years, but they were strictly voice only; they did not have the immediacy of video conversation.

About six or seven minutes into the conversation our local suburb experienced 'load shedding', when our electric power was cut off due to the power supply outage. The load shedding took us by surprise. Then, using a battery-powered cell phone, we reconnected over the internet and continued the conversation.

Even though the lights and computer were off and we were in the dark, we remained in the flow of the conversation and in communion as spiritually connected souls together.

As we connect to others who are also in tune with their soul, we become part of the global network that is uplifting consciousness. I find it improves the quality of my life to continue to maintain a connection with others who are also enlightened. There is a blessing that I share when I am associated with an invisible web of communion.

We now live in a house filled with 'Wi-Fi' connections. It wasn't too long ago when it seemed impossible to have a phone or computer and be connected to vast amounts of media without a cable to carry the information. Yet today my cell phone and computer connect automatically over Wi-Fi.

Likewise, we can also consciously be on-line and automatically connected energetically if we are open to it. We can then live in an environment where people care about each other and are concerned with sharing a higher vibration in a way that uplifts life.

I find it valuable to be conscious that I'm part of something larger than myself. I'm not just an isolated individual having an individual experience; rather, I am part of a global awakening that leads to a collective growth in perspective and understanding.

14

Spiritual Interest

I am interested in a philosophy that is not just inherited cultural dogma, or one based on pre-packaged beliefs, thoughts and opinions. Rather, the philosophy comes through an association that is creative, built on discovery and new experience. We can learn to be part of a network together, connected in a life- enhancing way.

To have comprehension and understanding requires ongoing interest. In 1979, researchers did an experiment where they wrote a story about a baseball game and gave it to a group of people to read. When they completed reading the baseball story, they then asked questions about it. They found a big difference in how people answered. Some people had a very clear memory of the game while other people could remember very little about the story.[32]

Then they asked participants if they were interested in baseball. Those who followed the sport could remember the baseball game described in the story very clearly. Their interest in baseball made it easy to recall the details of the game. Whereas the people who had no interest in baseball could hardly remember a thing about what they had just read. They did not have a grasp of the basics of baseball and could not imagine the game. It is the same in any field of our lives, including in our spiritual and philosophic experience. The stronger our foundation, the easier it is to grasp something that is new in that field.

To further our experience with new understanding and perspective requires continued participation. There are times when I read literature that is inspiring, yet I did not fully grasp it. The first time I read it, I didn't pick up on all the points, and missed out on some of the implications. When I read it again, I then had more insight.

Then if I reread the material a third time, it came more alive. It is interesting to acknowledge that with additional readings I gain a perspective that I hadn't seen when I initially looked at it. I find that my understanding builds over time because at a subconscious level I have had time to integrate the material, so that the next time I read it I have a foundation on which to build.

When we have an ongoing interest in philosophic or spiritual considerations, we establish a foundation of understanding. This participation includes reading books, blogs, weekly newsletters, attending lectures or religious services. If there is an openness of perspective when we consider inspirational material, it adds to what we already know. This will occur as long as we have an open mind and do not have a fixed view based on what we knew before. We will then better understand what is conveyed, and be able to apply it in our living, because it fits.

15

Philosophic Vision

In his book, *The Blank Slate*, Steven Pinker develops the idea of having a 'utopian vision' or a 'tragic vision'. I would like to explore these two perspectives and take them further.

Most of the time we may not be aware which kind of vision we have. Some political philosophers construct a utopian vision, thinking that a perfect political government can be achieved in a rational way. They do that by picturing a utopian society, even though there may be a huge gap between the envisioned utopia and the lives people live.

The utopian vision always thinks that life is getting better; it is an optimistic view of reality. Optimists have a belief in achieving utopia, but their lived experience may be very different as they struggle along. Their followers may have to cope with deceit, lies, compromises and nastiness that comes when their utopia is not realized. It is common for politicians to express idealized political beliefs full of promises and then find that they are mired in compromise.

The alternative is a tragic vision that envisions a bleak future in which everything goes wrong. This vision is based on the limitations and flaws inherent in a situation and may even predict the end of humanity through economic collapse, disease, nuclear war or climate change. This tragic vision is suspicious of people, their intentions, and predicts that the future will be worse than it is now.

The tragic vision is cautious; it thinks that bad things are going to happen in the future and there is nothing that can be done about it. It does not see the possibility of change and transformation. Rather, it focuses on evidence that things are deteriorating. People with this view can describe in detail the decline and predict catastrophe, yet are unable to imagine an alternative to change the course of events.

It is not a matter of having a picture in your mind of how perfect things could be or how bad things are becoming. It is not to be a prophet of either utopia or tragedy, both of which reflect a vision based on external events. There is a third alternative, which is to see clearly by having a spiritually inspired 'philosophic' vision. Then, regardless of the issues, there is an ability to express a higher quality of vision and clarity into the world and adapt.

What we see is not defined by a theory that we have learned. Rather, we see how to express in a way that has insight and is uplifting to other people. We can develop the capacity to attune to a higher quality of experience which results in a different outcome. Then we are not only forming a picture in our minds of what is outside ourselves, but also see with wisdom, gratitude and an openness to change.

It is a very different quality of perspective when a person is attuned in a way that creates a quality of expression that is life enhancing. Our seeing becomes an act of transmission that is creative and uplifts the world around us. Carl Jung said, "Who looks on the outside dreams, who looks on the inside awakens."[33] We need to perceive what is going on with our soul so as to understand what is happening on the inside, at the core of ourselves.

We think that dreaming only happens when we are asleep. Unfortunately, many people are living a nightmare. We are here, not to dream a different dream, rather to be awake and actually know what is going on in a vibrational sense.

16

Discovering the Truth

In January 2020 there was an Impeachment Trial of the President in the United States Senate. Via satalite broadcast, I as able to watch the trial from my home halfway across the world on CNN (Cable News Network). This would have been impossible in every other era in history. If I went back 100 years in time, and described that while sitting in my living room in Cape Town, I could watch a screen showing events taking place the United States Capitol, Washington D.C. as they were occurring, people would have thought that impossible and way beyond the realms of imagination.

There was a great debate in the US Senate as to whether additional witnesses should be cross-examined, or whether the cross-examination should be stopped and the impeachment put to a vote. The view on one side was that any judicial process should include cross-examination – the thought was that with cross-examination the truth would be discovered. The other side of the house thought it would be an unnecessary repetition of the previous debate in the House of Representatives, as each side had their preexisting prejudice.

The idea that debate can lead to the truth is not a recent one. It dates back to ancient Greek philosophers such as Socrates and Plato, who believed in using debate and dialectic to discover the truth. Socrates was concerned that if they did not debate, their philosophy would be crystallized. The thinking at that time was that if the philosophy was no longer questioned through debate, the truth would not be discovered.

So, one way of discovering the truth is through questioning and debate. This is used in court rooms across the world and is an accepted way of discovering the truth. If there is no debate the philosophy can get stuck in fixed positions as there is no space for the truth to be explored.

An alternative to asking questions and debating, the truth can be discovered through stillness. Rather than having thoughts going around in our heads, there can be a focus on stillness and meditation. This is a way of discovering the truth that is not based on dialectical debate, but through individual centering and meditation. This form of stillness and meditation has been used in Buddhism and other forms of religion. It includes listening, pondering, mindfulness, awareness and focus to engender an enhanced experience of clarity.

Each of these two approaches is valid, in that either can be used to come to new perspective and understanding.

A third approach in discovering the truth is through the tonal quality behind what is said. The truth is discovered through a tonal harmonization, in that it extends beyond the spoken words in a similar way that chant, song or prayer are used. For the truth to be manifest it is necessary to develop a quality of relatedness through a collective atmosphere where the truth is discovered and experienced. As there is an uplifting tone to what is said, that is shared by all concerned. By knowing and sharing an uplifting tone there is greater fluidity for the truth to emerge.

A fourth approach is that truth can also be discovered through collective worship. When the worshipers generate the atmosphere or the spiritual aura as a group, they can gain new insight and understanding. The participants then experience the truth in a way that is resonant and inspired so that there is collective illumination. This is a discovery of the truth not only through a shared mental illumination, but through a spiritual illumination. It is not just the thoughts or lack of thought, but the shared enlightenment that brings understanding.

We can use all these methods of discovering the truth to create a philosophically inspired life that is worth living.

17

Preparing

Nelson Mandela, the iconic South African leader, was interviewed by Tony Robbins. "How did you survive 27 years in prison?" asked Robbins, to which Mandela replied, "I didn't survive, I prepared."[34]

Even though Mandela was in prison he was preparing for what came next, which is a remarkable way of seeing things as he achieved unimaginable greatness in his later years, becoming a world icon and inspiring a nation to change.

I was considering what it is to be active in one's senior years in the context of the 2020 American Presidential Election. A number of candidates were over the age of 70, even though none had the wisdom, vision or stature of Mandela. Some of us aspire to continue creating our future as elders; to be active and engaged, rather than giving up and retiring into a boring routine. Others, as they get older, are digging a hole that leads to the grave. Rather than surviving isolated and alone, it is possible to live as part of a whole, participating in a larger community.

It is common for those in their teens and 20s to feel inadequate and anxious, because they are not yet able to access their full inner potency and live with wisdom. Our capacity for wisdom and understanding grows as we age. It requires that we do the work of spiritually aligning and learning so that we continue to grow in stature. In the continuing process of maturing, we become more spiritually potent. Mandela is an example of one who reached his full potential in his 70s.

There is continued growth and development that comes in staying in the process of taking responsibility for personal spiritual practice. Responsibility sounds like a burden, but it actually lifts our spirit and gives us an elevated mood.

We may find ourselves in the usual routine that most people engage in, earning an income while also taking care of family or friends, but we also have a philosophic responsibility as well. When we live in the context of our philosophy we grow as a person and have an uplifting effect on others. As we continue to prepare spiritually, and become more in tune with our soul, we discover new ranges of inner satisfaction.

18

The Shift Towards Writing and Creating

In the book, "Smarter than you Think", Clive Thompson[35] notes that in recent years the amount of communication using writing has increased significantly. Many are unaware that this has happened. When I was growing up, the only way to send an instant written message was using a postal telegram. Most correspondence to family, friends and for business was written and sent via the post office. Letters for business were typed, whereas it was more common for personal correspondence to family and friends to be handwritten.

Excluding bills and financial statements, it was unusual for an individual to receive more than a few letters a month, unless they were a very active correspondent. By contrast, the average person's email box in this era, fills up rapidly. For those in business, according to The Guardian, the average office worker gets 121 emails per day, and some get many more than that.[36] Email has become quite a chore for many of us, and at times it may seem overwhelming.

Before the digital era, most writing of stories, news and information was for commercial benefit or associated with academic institutions. Writing and creating content was mostly done to earn income through publishing it in newspapers, books and magazines which were widely read. Other than a few 'letters to the editor' there was very little interaction with the writer.

Since the start of the internet, there has been a staggering growth in the amount of writing. Initially, most saw the internet as an electronic version of traditional media, and as the bandwidth increased there would be more communication via video. Instead, it changed in unexpected ways. The amount of shared written content and comment multiplied exponentially as the internet improved the ease of sharing. By writing, the writer becomes more engaged and is no longer a passive viewer. Previously, it was more common to read books and magazines as a consumer of content, than to create your own, but this has changed. Since the year 2 000, in the new millennium there is less reading of books, magazines and articles and there is much more interaction using new media platforms. The big shift is towards writing and creating content that can be shared on-line, as more and more people are posting their interests, opinions, insights, experiences and visual images on-line. Unfortunately, some also share nastiness!

Electronic word processing made it easy to write and edit work. Millions of people are active on-line, writing and creating content, sharing photo's, ideas and opinions. They are using a range of media, including email, WhatsApp, Twitter, Facebook, Texting, Instagram, and blogs, and see the value of these platforms to share their ideas and opinions and also comment on the posts of others.

Consider using writing to encourage, show care and uplift consciousness. That is using writing to promote change and to connect in a wholesome way. When we write in a way that entertains, informs, offers insight, expresses appreciation, or moves a project forward, then writing is a way to make the world a better place.

19

A Resonant Tone

Yo-Yo Ma's cello playing carries a rich resonance. At the start of 2020 he traveled around the world playing in 36 iconic venues across the globe as part of The Bach Suites Project. In Cape Town he played at Kirstenbosch National Botanical Gardens to an audience of more than 7000 people who were transfixed, listening to his resonant solo performance, giving him a standing ovation.

He is a musician with vision, mastery and skill who makes the music come alive in a magical way. He spoke in an interview about "Bach's ability to speak to our common humanity at a time when our civic conversation is often focused on division."[37] He also spoke about transcending technique when performing, so that the quality of expression is more than just playing the notes. His playing inspires us to not live our lives in a narrow way and miss the opportunity for a finer quality of expression.

Nikola Tesla said, "...if you want to find the secrets of the universe, think in terms of energy, frequency and vibration."[38] He could have added the word 'resonance'. When one listens to Yo-Yo Ma playing the cello, one has an experience of energy, frequency and vibration through his deeply resonant playing. Each one of us also has an ability to use our body to express energy, frequency and vibration in a resonant way that is in tune with our soul, that transforms our experience.

The transmission of content and information through frequency and vibration has grown exponentially using electronics, in a way that could not have been imagined in times past. It is technology that harnesses frequency and vibration and compresses it into a digital form.

In his book, *Smarter Than You Think*, Clive Thompson wrote, "When British anthropologist Robin Dunbar studied everyday, face-to-face conversation in Britain, he found that people spend fully 65% of the time talking about themselves and other people."[39] That is what most people do. We can ask ourselves if we are just sharing opinions about people, or if we are uplifting the frequency and vibration. If conversation is opinionated and nasty, it lowers the tone.

After watching the movie, *Bombshell*, about TV

news anchor Megyn Kelly and how Fox News treated women, I saw Megyn being interviewed by talk show host, Bill Maher. She made the point that the internet can bring out the worst version of ourselves. When Megyn Kelly was critical of Donald Trump as a presidential candidate, she found herself under attack during the 2016 election. She indicated that it took courage just to be at work and do her job in a professional way, and not take these attacks personally. She said that at the time she reminded herself that "it's not about me, it's about the audience and the truth."[40]

This is a remarkable statement considering how many conversations that people have are about themselves and the opinions they have about other people, rather than a concern for the truth. They may go on about how they are suffering and being victimized and how nasty they think other people are, but that is not inspiring.

The alternative is to have a way of thinking that is not about yourself, but about what you express in an authentic way that uplifts and transforms. When we become aware of the tone of what we are saying and express at a higher frequency, it is 'not about us', but about uplifting the field we live in.

20

It Takes Practice

I once received a YouTube ad offering singing coaching. It was obviously sent to the wrong person, as I cannot sing in tune and was not looking for singing coaching! But the coach gave the assurance that they could teach almost anybody to sing if they did the course diligently and practiced regularly. To improve performance required practice, including singing scales every day and various voice exercises to develop the throat muscles. To make progress, a student has to do the daily exercises and follow the coaching.

Those with natural ability start singing at a young age and will get better if they continue singing when they grow up. Some who do not have a natural ability, sing off pitch and are out of tune. Watch any talent show on TV and you will hear aspiring singers who don't have the ability to sing in tune; they haven't been fortunate to have received coaching or done the hours of practice.

Research conducted on English choral singers at Canterbury Christ Church University[41] found that the singers experience joy when singing and that they enjoyed singing more than they enjoyed listening to music. If they had asked young soccer players if they enjoyed playing soccer more than watching a soccer match, they would probably have had the same result.

The choral singers have the right muscle tone and control to sing in tune because they practice singing regularly. In any sport, including soccer, the top players play almost every day and have a coach. They obviously love playing soccer and play for hours on end, but to improve they also need to be willing to follow the coach's instructions.

It takes constant practice to bring the qualities of grace, stability, humanity and understanding into our lives. When we are stressed and feeling the pressure of challenging circumstances, if we've practiced these qualities, we will have the ability and strength to express them. People may think they can do it without practicing, but it doesn't go as well when they are under pressure or feeling stressed.

In whatever circumstances we find ourselves, there will be opportunities to care and practice the expression of love. If we don't consciously practice acting in a way that is loving, caring and spiritually inspired, it may not come naturally. The world will be a better place if we develop our spiritual potential, continue to be spiritually resonant and express the higher vibration of love in our daily life.

In whatever circumstances we find ourselves, there will be opportunities to practice living in tune with our soul. If we continue to consciously practice living in tune with our soul, we will have a life filled with loving and caring. Living in tune with our soul may not come naturally. Through reading spiritually inspiring literature and by attending lectures and services, we practice being in tune with our soul. It makes a significant difference if we continue to be spiritually resonant with our soul and carry a harmonious vibration in our daily life.

21

Difficulty and Harmony

On 11 February 2020 the founder of the choral group Ladysmith Black Mambazo, Joseph Shabalala, passed away. Ladysmith Black Mambazo became known internationally after collaborating with Paul Simon on his 1986 album, *Graceland*. The group sang on the track 'Diamonds on the Soles of her Shoes' with Simon.

When Paul Simon went to Africa searching for a new direction in his music, he discovered Joseph Shabalala who had been creating music for over 20 years. What Simon found most fascinating was that Ladysmith Black Mambazo came from a very different musical tradition. The group didn't use sheet music or notate their songs in the way that is done in the West, as Shabalala had very little formal education. He used a different musical framework and created an entirely different sound that resonated with a worldwide audience.

Shabalala created this new sound despite impoverished circumstances. It was a pattern of harmony and rhythm unlike anything that had gone before, although it was influenced by traditional Zulu *isicathamiya* harmonies, which Paul Simon found remarkable.[42] There was no precedence for the way they performed or the sound they created. Using bass notes contrasted with higher notes, their acappella singing wove the sound together in a unique way.

By the turn of the 21st century, the group had recorded more than 30 albums, establishing it as the best-selling musical group in Africa.[43] It was Shabalala's imagination that created this new sound. As he said in 2008, "We have been awarded five Grammy Awards, represented our homeland of South Africa at many prestigious events, including accompanying Nelson Mandela to Norway to receive the Nobel Peace Prize; traveled the world so many times and most importantly, spread a message of peace, love and harmony to millions of people."[44] It was the use of harmony in the music that was so attractive.

Sometimes we may find ourselves in difficult circumstances and yet even with limitations, we can still be creative and, like Joseph Shabalala, express harmony.

Consider that we have more creativity in us than

we give ourselves credit for, but it takes application. Every day we have the opportunity to live in harmony, to create out of nothing and to express our vision, just as Joseph Shabalala did.

22

It Isn't Smooth

I used to think that my life would go smoothly as an easy forward progression. However, I have found many unanticipated twists and turns. My life looks like a stock market graph; it has little ups and downs all the time, as well as larger cycles of change, some lasting many years.

Scientific progress is based on an assumption that through predicting outcomes, we can create a better future. Many are living a vastly better lifestyle thanks to scientific advances.[45] Yet scientific research often detects randomness in the results of experimental data and there are many outcomes that science cannot predict.

When mathematician Gottfried Wilhelm Leibniz was in the process of developing Calculus in the 1670s, he thought that progress was smooth,[46] making it easy to predict the tipping point when change happens. His thinking at that time was that "the world is continuous and unbroken; nature does not make jumps but always moves smoothly",[47] and that calculus would be able to predict the rate and direction of change.

Yet change is often unanticipated, it is not easy to predict the direction or rate-of-change. In stock markets, educated investors and analysts looking at the financial indicators may predict that based on economic indicators that a change will happen. Yet their track record will show that it's very difficult to accurately forecast the exact time when the market changes direction to turn upward or downward. Similarly, in our own lives, even with the best insight or intentions, we may know that change is coming, but then get the timing wrong.

It is impossible to make our lives smooth without them becoming dull and boring. Living a dull and boring life may be worse than coping with variation and change. There is joy in overcoming setbacks. A triumph over adversity generates resilience. We need challenge and change to make us grow. We feel alive when we are actively engaged in exploring and living a more fulfilling life.

23

Spiritual Capital

It is common for people to think that they will receive a spiritual download in a flash of inspiration. That with an instant flash they will awaken, have insight and be wise forever. The view is that, as result of the incredible experience they have had in spiritually awakening, the rest of their lives will go well.

But for most people that isn't the case; the flash of inspiration is just a starting point of awakening to a longer spiritual journey. Spiritual growth is incremental and there are many steps to finding spiritual alignment that occur over a period of time.

In modern business management the word 'capital' has been extended past its common use as *financial capital*, which is monetary wealth, to other forms of capital, namely human capital and *social capital*. Individuals strengthen their *human capital* through education and experience. Through *social capital* we develop connections and networks that are also valuable over time.

Consider that we can also grow our *spiritual capital* as we continue to spiritually align, connect and maintain our inner harmony. Generating spiritual capital also requires spiritual participation over a lifetime. Our *spiritual capital* grows as we continue our spiritual considerations and find inner harmony, even when it feels intense or uncomfortable to do so. The key is to not lose one's temper, become self-righteous or reactive. Instead, we can keep generating *spiritual capital* when we stay in the process and maintain our focus.

Investment advisors always say that the best growth in wealth occurs when you save and invest consistently over a long period of time. Small investments over a long period of time usually out-perform one single big investment. The same is true in the generation of *spiritual capital*: ongoing participation generates the greatest return.

Our spiritual growth will be limited if we react, form judgments, make everyone else wrong, hang on to old beliefs or refuse to go further in the process. What is required is an ongoing openness to the unfolding truth. When we maintain our inner harmony what continues to emerge is learning, increased understanding and fresh perspective.

Over and over again, I have seen people get to a

point where their spiritual awakening is moving forward, but through a difficult circumstance or disagreement they retreat to an old way of thinking and say, "They're wrong and I'm out of here." If they had stayed in the process and held steady, despite their view of whatever was happening and then focused on rediscovering their inner harmony, they would generate more *spiritual capital.*

No matter what is going on in the world or what people say to you, it becomes a habit to:

- focus on meaning at the soul level,
- find spiritual alignment in tune with your soul
- consider acting with wisdom and care

As we stay in the process and are open to continually taking additional small steps, our spiritual experience comes from knowing inner harmony, rather than just a belief or theory. Then our understanding is based on a stability of experience that is able to carry us through, no matter what challenges we may face.

24

Tired of War

In March 2020, the United States reached a peace deal with the Taliban in Afghanistan. President Trump said he had faith in the deal because "everybody is just tired of war." [48] After 18 years since the conflict began, this sentiment is understandable. In Afghanistan, the springtime was seen differently from the rest of the world as it was the start of the fighting season after the long, cold winter. Year after year they would wait until spring to start fighting again. This peace deal started the process that led to the American withdrawal from Afghanistan a year and a half later.

It was thought at the time that the Afghans could not face another season of fighting after 18 years of conflict and were ready to negotiate a peaceful alternative. In our own lives we do not have to fight for years on end, only to find peace after enduring many years of suffering.

Having a self-righteous conviction that other people are wrong and that the only way to bring about change is through fighting, even if it means fighting to the death, is destructive. That is the way it's been throughout the history of humanity.

It's very easy to get involved in self-deception thinking one is right and then get into a fight. This brings suffering in a situation as it is often a false interpretation of the facts. This deception is madness because the consequences of fighting are not considered. War between countries and nations is a collective psychosis where destructive violence is justified. In a battle, all sides suffer casualties and damage.

How do we find peace? Consider that peace originates through an experience of inner harmony. There is no peace when fighting for territory, political beliefs or any other personal views. Peace does not come through trying to dominate other people, or boosting the ego, or aiming to attain wealth and prestige at all costs. Peace comes through resonance with the source of all peace and a love for life.

If one feels the urge towards peace, one can ask oneself if this 'urge' is really 'urgent'. When battle begins, revenge and anger take over and become more urgent than peace. The desire for peace gets forgotten when the focus is to retaliate through a reign of terror. When we make sharing the experience of a higher state of peace more 'urgent' than revenge, it will allow us to engage in shared dialogue which opens up the possibility for the conflict to be transformed.

For some, it takes courage to express love and to be loved because that is not what they do regularly, but it takes no courage to express anger. Expressing love should be an easy thing to do, yet some people find it very hard.

If it were easy to express peace and harmony, more people would do it and there would be a lot more peace and less violence in the world. It takes wisdom to engage in a loving way. It is not easy to be open and vulnerable, to give up thinking that one is always right, and instead to consider alternative perspectives while still holding core values.

Peace does not come from the outside in; it comes from the inside out. We generate a peaceful atmosphere when we are in tune with our soul. We are then open to love and understanding. When we experience a quality of inner peace and harmony ourselves, we can then share that with other people.

25

The Imaginary Box

It is common to feel constrained by limitations and feel restricted as if in an imaginary box. Then the view is that violence is necessary to smash a way out of the box. Alternatively, an experience of inner harmony and friendship gets us out of the box. There will also be situations where to stay out of the box we were in, the wise thing to do is to walk away and never look back.

There are many who have suffered because they loved in a naive way and that love was abused. They may feel they were taken advantage of, or encountered aggression. They may then retreat and have a view that to be open and loving is a weakness. There are times to take a stand to protect oneself, align with higher purpose and not allow bullying. With a foundation in tune with our soul we become strong enough to love again. We are then able to release our hurt and share at a soul level with another trustworthy person.

Just sustaining one loving relationship over many years takes caring, perseverance, compromise and an openness to change. It includes creating a space where the truth is heard on both sides.

There is always the opportunity to be more connected with other people in an auric way, aura to aura, sharing the aura of love. Then our lives become not just about us individually, but about the auric field that is shared together. This can be shared in the immediate environment or can be shared as a connection across the globe. It may seem unimaginable, but there are no constraints to sharing the aura of love, which is not limited by geographic location or the box we may be in.

26

Choosing the Right Pill

In a scene in the 1999 film, *The Matrix*, rebel leader Morpheus offers the main character, Neo, the choice between a red pill and a blue pill.

The *blue pill* represents a beautiful prison that will lead him back to ignorance, living in confined comfort without want or fear. The *red pill* is a harsher and more difficult choice as it represents an uncertain future. It would free him from the enslaving control of the machine-generated dream world and allow him to escape into the real world, living 'the truth of reality'.[49]

In the movie, Neo chooses the *red pill*.

I learned many years ago about the mathematical concept of a matrix: an array of numbers in a grid that are governed by a formula. As the formula changes, the information in the matrix changes. This field of mathematics influences some of the work done on computers and the internet in the transmission of data and pictures.

A mathematical matrix is a collection of what are called vectors; a vector is a quantity having 'magnitude' well as 'direction'. When we choose the *blue pill* option of comfort and ignorance, we lose our direction; we compromise our lives and find ourselves restricted and controlled by our own missed opportunities, other people, the media or our beliefs. Without even realizing it, our lives become narrow, dull and boring.

It is possible to live a life that has magnitude and direction; that is, choosing the *red pill*, even if initially there is risk and difficulty in living with the 'truth of reality'. Recognize that if there is no direction to your life and also no magnitude, then you have a narrow, shallow existence. Having direction and magnitude in what we are expressing radiates outwards and makes our life more interesting.

When an individual is closed off and narrow, their life can become a struggle and they may suffer in a variety of ways. They can tell you all about the suffering, but the choice they have made is for the *blue pill* of ignorance and comfort. The question is whether they have the courage and are open to choosing the *red pill*, with all its risks, that will lift them out of the state they are in.

One might ask, "Do you want a life with direction and magnitude?" When one listens carefully, it's remarkable how quickly people will tell you about the bad choices they have made, yet they lack the courage to do anything about it and suffer as a result.

By making the more difficult choice, we can live life through developing our wisdom so that we are no longer unconsciously sabotaging ourselves by making bad choices. Many choose the *blue pill* option of immediate comfort and then find themselves trapped in limitations. They think that there's not very much they can do about their situation, so they persist in those attitudes in a dogged way.

The *red pill* option seems risky at first. One may feel vulnerable – as one is stepping out of one's comfort zone. It is a choice that leads to playing in a higher level matrix and over time, it leads to a better outcome. Even if it initially seems more difficult, the *red pill* option allows us to choose a life where we continue to grow in magnitude. The magnitude comes as we bring a finer quality of expression based on our inner sense of harmony.

The magnitude of what we have taken on may cause some discomfort. But when we have inner harmony, our problems diminish in size. Then we are able to live an enlightened life, and creatively overcome the issues we face. Choosing the *red pill* is not always comfortable, but it leads to a life of greater magnitude and direction.

27

Five Types of Wisdom

I know people who on a regular basis face difficulties, struggles, hardship and strife. One of the main causes of their suffering is a lack of wisdom, although they may put the blame elsewhere. Wisdom is vital if our lives are going to move forward creatively to live an interesting life.

There are also consequences when we live reactively, doing and saying whatever we feel like. We will encounter difficulties by living without an underlying wisdom. There are five types of wisdom, and we need all of them:

Ancient Wisdom: This is wisdom we receive from writings and teachings from the past. There is ancient wisdom in all religions and philosophies that has been passed down through the centuries. Rather than discarding ancient wisdom as being out of date, we should explore how it applies in our lives today.

Accepted Wisdom: This is what the people around you—the community, elders, parents or friends—

acknowledge to be true. It is an understanding that is generally accepted as wisdom in your community, as it may have been helpful in the past.

With the rate of change in the modern world, what was accepted wisdom may encounter changes in technology and social norms. Often teenagers and twenty-somethings challenge the accepted wisdom of their parents, as they find the world has changed and they are facing challenges that didn't exist before.

Accumulated Wisdom: This is the wisdom that we gain throughout our lives by trial and error and by taking a few hard knocks. As we face difficulties and find creative solutions, we hopefully acquire wisdom over time, although not everyone applies this wisdom or learns from their mistakes. Lacking wisdom, some people repeat mistakes over and over again and don't learn the lessons. This may seem incomprehensible to a friend, mentor or counselor.

Wisdom in the moment: This is wisdom that we apply in the moment. It includes:

- The wisdom to speak, or to be silent.
- The wisdom to change, adapt or hold firm.
- The wisdom to be take action or be patient.
- The wisdom to challenge or back off.

This type of wisdom has a significant impact on our relationships and our working lives. Managing people in an organization often requires wisdom in the moment when confronted with an issue, or when circumstances change.

Flexible Wisdom: This is:

- Wisdom that has a sensitivity
- Wisdom that has understanding
- Wisdom that has perspective
- Wisdom to be open to change.

Having wisdom is sometimes seen as a fixed perspective, that has all the answers with a clear vision of what the next step is. What we are considering is a quality of wisdom based on flexibility that has an openness to change to better navigate the way forward. Wisdom comes to us as we live in tune with our soul.

Wisdom is not just having great ideas and keeping them to yourself. It includes having interest in other people and in finding a way to articulate whatever wisdom we wish to bring into a situation, so as to uplift circumstances and improve the lives of others.

All these types of wisdom depend on our emotional maturity. Applying these types of wisdom must be done in a way that is relevant. It is a wisdom based in a desire to serve others rather than being clever or trying to impress. If we quote from the past, it must be fitting and appropriate so that it adds to what is emerging and is applicable and is enhancing for everybody.

Having these types of wisdom allows us to elevate our lives, helping us navigate our way through ever-changing circumstances.

28

The Flow State

In his audio book, *Mapping Cloud Nine,*[50] Steven Kotler describes a flow state in the context of sporting, business or scientific achievement, where somebody comes into a state of flow and achieves something extraordinary. Let us consider the experience of living in a flow state as an internally aligned experience.

One of the examples Kotler uses in describing a flow state is world-leading skateboard jumper, Danny Way, who skates down steep ramps and then jumps into the air before landing on a ramp on the other side. According to Kotler, Danny Way can do this because he experiences a state of flow when jumping. Way's greatest achievement was jumping over the Great Wall of China; a massive jump of over 70 feet.

Such a jump takes great courage. Danny Way may have experienced an extraordinary few moments of flow so as to successfully make the jump. The flow he experienced may be confined to being in an altered state when skating and jumping, whereas I am considering the state of flow in every aspect of our lives.

The idea of spiritual flow is not a new one. Throughout history, Hinduism, Buddhism, Taoism and Islamic Sufism have all touched on this type of experience in some way. A state of being at one with all things is regarded as a state of flow.

In their book, *Flow: the psychology of optimal experience*, authors Nakamura and Csíkszentmihályi[51] identify some factors in the experience of flow:

- An intense concentration in the present moment.
- The merging of awareness and action.
- A loss of reflective self-consciousness.
- A sense of control.
- The subjective experience of time is altered.
- Experiencing the activity as intrinsically rewarding.

These describe a state of spiritual flow where we don't lose our sense of self-awareness; rather, it becomes expanded.

"In yogic traditions such as Raja Yoga reference is made to a state of flow in the practice of Samyama, a psychological absorption in the object of meditation".[52]

There are many ways to speak about the state of flow, but what they are describing is an experience where one is spiritually aligned and in control in a focused way.

Spiritual knowing comes from the experience of flow, not the other way around. Flow is a positive and enjoyable experience. When experiencing that flow, it brings a feeling of happiness. One is not trying to experience flow to get something, but rather from that flow comes wisdom. That is, having a sense of inner clarity that brings intrinsic motivation.

This is a sense of flow while dealing with ordinary situations in whatever way they come to us. In a state of flow, we have a sense of spiritual attunement that is different from the normal human experience.

In the flow state there is no experience of alienation, inadequacy, low self-esteem or anxiety. There is a knowing that comes from the flow state, which is a different inner identity. Flow can also be experienced by engaging in spiritual connection and philosophic inquiry, so as to be in tune with the soul.

No one can generate a state of flow for us. We individually play a part in resonantly aligning with the flow state. When we are in a spiritually flowing state, we have a different perspective and feel more internally aligned and connected.

29

Protective Providence

There is a philosophy that some people subscribe to that all that is required is to live in the present moment. But this philosophy ignores the concept of providence, which dates back to Thomas Aquinas, a priest who was born in Italy, in 1225.[53] Providence is described in the Oxford Language Dictionary either as the 'protective care of God' or as a 'timely preparation for future eventualities.' Providence provides protection in the present and for the future.[54]

Consider that as we live in the present moment with providence, there are two things going on in the background:

1.We are doing things that create the future out of the present.

2.We are also able to cope with the unexpected future: those circumstances that we did not see coming and are not prepared for.

Providence reminds us that what we do in the

present has an impact on the future, so we cannot live recklessly. Living in the present does not mean that we are not considering the future at the same time. It is weak strategy to live in a reckless or naive way, as we are creating the future in the present moment all the time. We create the whole spectrum of the future, from the immediate future to the long-term future, by what we do in the present.

In a TED Talk in 2015, five years before the outbreak of the Covid pandemic, Bill Gates predicted the possibility of a viral pandemic and warned that countries of the world were unprepared for the next epidemic.[55] Given how difficult it is to predict the future five years in advance, that Bill Gates made this prediction shows insight that few have. It could be why he is one of the richest men on earth, in that he can foresee events years into the future! But he didn't predict the date that the pandemic would occur. All he predicted was that a pandemic could happen at some time in the future.

When the Covid virus struck, the world was indeed unprepared. There was panic, as nation after nation went into lockdown, meaning that people had to stay at home and only go out to shop for basic needs. People lined up in long 'socially distant' queues, wearing face masks to go shopping. Many were desperate to buy hand sanitizer, masks, disinfectant and food. None of the world's governments took sufficient precautionary steps to ensure there were sufficient supplies beforehand.

As we are aligned with spirit, there is protective care. That is not to say we won't get sick; everybody was at risk in the pandemic. But when we are spiritually aligned, we are able to be intelligent in any situation and have a sense of protection, even if illness or unexpected circumstances take us by surprise. No one could have seen how the Covid virus would affect all of humanity. But when we are spiritually aligned, the way that we deal with unexpected change is not based in fear or anguish or feeling that life is unfair, but rather in knowing that we are supported by providence. The sense of providence gives us the strength and understanding to deal with whatever comes. We then inherently know that we can overcome the challenge that is in front of us by intelligently investigating the situation and then having an openness to take the next step.

Change comes when we are open to possibility – not just trusting it will all work out, but rather playing our part in the change. That is seeing what is accurate and what fits. Then we can take action. It is having the wisdom to discern what is occurring in an emotionally intelligent way, so that we are open to receiving and adapting to new information.

Often when change happens, our survival comes not out of fear, but rather from having understanding, perspective, flexibility and a willingness to change. When we align with our core truth we are in a better position take the next step. When we have adverse experiences in life, the experience of providence comes when we have taken care of the philosophical fundamentals and are thus in a position do what is necessary in order to adapt.

30

An Authentic Picture

I found a box of childhood pictures, previously known as 'Kodak moments', and it was nice to see what I looked like back then. Future generations won't know what a Kodak moment is, as all picture-taking has gone digital and photographic film has mostly disappeared. We now mostly take pictures using our cell phones.

Photographers, when using photographic film in a studio, had skill to arrange the image by setting up the background and adjusting the lighting. This would make the picture look more impactful. In the modern digital age, altering a picture has become much easier. It can be 'photoshopped' and digitally manipulated in many different ways, including changing the background and varying the dimensions of the image, removing imperfections and flaws or inserting a new image.

This has become an issue because the pictures we see in magazines aren't real anymore. A model will be photographed wearing a fashionable outfit and then the image is adjusted to make her thinner and sexier, without any skin blemishes. Or the background may be changed to a totally different location. But a photoshopped picture lacks authenticity. The pictures become unreal because we don't live in a perfect, photoshopped world. We have to accept reality the way it is, even if it isn't perfect.

A few years ago, photo editors in magazines were worried that the truth in photos was dying, but the reverse is also happening because people are starting to mock photographs for their inauthenticity. If the photographs no longer represent the truth, they become a joke. Artificially created images are now seen to be inauthentic and fake.[56]

When TV comedians, such as Trevor Noah or Bill Maher, joke about politicians,[57] you realize how easily politicians' inauthenticity can be exposed. Dwelling on the negatives of a politician is one of the comedians' tools of the trade. We can laugh because we realize that many politicians are projecting a false image. Some politicians are masters at creating a facade that appears to be genuine, while actually having a hidden agenda. They may appear to be supporting the poor and disadvantaged, but when it comes to a vote on legislation, they favor large wealthy corporations, corrupt practices and vested interests.

Instead of creating a superficial image, what we are looking for are opportunities for genuine interactions that are spiritually authentic. This is to be real at all levels, including the vibrational level. Then we can share at many levels rather than just looking good on the surface, while having an inadequate experience internally.

There are always ever-changing circumstances, and the challenge is to aim to be spiritually authentic despite constant change. There is always a new picture emerging. As the pace of life is increasing it's very easy to feel overwhelmed and negative about what is happening. The secret is to remember that we are here to transform the negatives into an uplifting, positive picture.

Some become so absorbed in the negatives that they don't see the spiritual opportunity. But there is an authenticity that comes when one is genuine from the inside outward. This is very different from creating an image that looks good on the outside but is rotten inside. Rather than living a pretend life like a photoshopped image, we can share a genuine quality interaction together. When we are spiritually genuine and in tune with our soul, we can enjoy spending time with other people who are also genuine. The world is filled with inauthenticity and image making, but we have a better life if we are interacting in a way that is authentic.

31

A Stoic Approach

In March 2020 the Covid-19 pandemic took the world by surprise. At first there was denial; people thought it was only spreading in China and would never reach around the world. There had been other viruses in recent decades, including SARS, Ebola and MERS, and the world got through those pandemics without too much disruption. This was surely going to be the same. Then the medical establishment discovered that this virus travels rapidly and remains undetected for a few days before symptoms manifest. The number of infections all over the world grew exponentially.

Initially, there was a lot of anxiety and panic as people rushed out and bought face masks and hand sanitizer. When people are panicking, frustrated and anxious, a Stoic philosophy is a good one to adopt. Stoicism dates back to the ancient Greek and Roman times and was adopted by Emperor Marcus

Aurelius.[58] The Stoic philosophy encourages us to not torture ourselves about the things we cannot control. Rather, to control our intentions, behavior and actions in a virtuous and wise way. The Stoics regarded living with virtue as rewarding.

The Stoic view is to use our time to let go of the old way of thinking and develop something new, while still retaining virtue by behaving in a way that is rational and responsible. During a lockdown, hedonism, the philosophy of the pursuit of pleasure, was not acceptable or allowed by law. We could not socialize or go out and party. Instead, it was a time to find tranquility; a time to be alone and in loneliness find a new sense of connection without personal contact.

The lockdown gave people an opportunity to re-look at their lives rather than be plunged into anxiety and depression. There was an opportunity to consider the four Stoic virtues of wisdom, morality, courage and moderation. A lockdown is a time for being isolated physically, but it also offered an opportunity for conscious connection in spirit. Some people found themselves experiencing loneliness, helplessness and feelings of disempowerment. These feelings can grow when people feel isolated. For some it takes courage to be alone. We had time to reflect on past relationships that broke down because of a lack of integrity, and time to consider how to repair them. Lockdown required us to adapt, to change and to accept things the way they were. It takes courage to connect while in restricted circumstances. There are many ways to be creative: hobbies, the arts, writing, cooking, reading or any other activity we may engage in. We could connect on-line in a way that throughout all of history was impossible until the internet was created and cell phones were widely available. It opened up new possibilities in how to share globally in a creative way while being confined at home.

A lockdown was a time to slow down and reflect. It was an opportunity to move past isolation, to the realization that one is never isolated spiritually. Even when alone physically, if one is engaged in philosophic consideration and doing soul work, one is not isolated. If we have a spiritual enquiry, we can reconstruct our lives in an authentic way with wisdom, morality and courage while living in moderation, which is a Stoic way of dealing with the situation.

32

The Disconnect

During load shedding, as experienced in South Africa, the amount of electricity consumed on the national electrical grid is reduced to match the amount of electricity that is generated. If the generation of electricity is less than the consumption, then the entire electrical grid can trip, resulting in a national power outage.

If there is a total blackout, it can take days to reboot the electrical grid and get the generation of electricity synchronized with the consumption. To protect the entire grid, some of the electricity supply to users, is shut down. The supply to various suburbs around the country is switched off for two hours at a time on a rotating basis according to a schedule to balance the generation to usage.

Likewise, we have to look at our generation in our personal lives. If we are overloaded, we have to shed some of the load. This is not just a physical load; we carry psychological load as well. The psychological load comes when we feel overwhelmed by all the things that are happening in our lives, our concerns and fears, and all the other events that we are aware of.

We are living at a time where we are receiving a lot more information, messages and entertainment than has been the case throughout history. We are connected through our phones and screens so that we receive instant news from friends and family, and also a vast amount of political and economic information from around the globe, which can be overwhelming.

What is required is shedding the load that we carry and focusing on generating spiritual flow. If we are generating spiritual flow, we are creating a capacity to manage psychological load. When we take time to generate spiritually and live in balance, we are in position to meet the load that comes to us. Since April 2008, electrical load shedding has occurred a number of times in South Africa. The procurement at the Electricity Supply Commission (ESKOM) has been corrupted and regular maintenance has declined. The frustration and inconvenience of power outages are the result of dishonesty and a lack of integrity on the part of the managers who have undermined the electricity supply.

Despite living at a time when most people are more

digitally connected than ever, some people feel disconnected from the family and local communities, as well as from what is going on in society and political activity. There is a feeling of frustration, but I would suggest that it's not just a political disconnect or, in South Africa's case, an electrical one, but that people are feeling a disconnect at the very core of themselves as they are out of tune with their soul. This is a spiritual disconnect, caused by a widespread lack of integrity and misalignment with the truth.

What I am considering is finding an authenticity of spiritual experience and that implies reconnecting at a fundamental level. That is, becoming more personally connected to truth so that one becomes authentic and ethical at the core of oneself. Then the truth is no longer a set of opinions or beliefs, but rather a lived experience of authentic spiritual understanding, caring and uplifting expression.

When we find ourselves connected to other people who are on the same spiritual grid, our relationships are more real and substantial. Authentic relationships are not always easy; they require maturity. If one is off key, personal honesty is needed to return to a state of resonance with one's core of truth.

When we take care of our spiritual generation and the atmosphere we live in, there is an experience of being blessed. Then we have a consciousness that is inspired by truth, and we can bring that into our current circumstances. Then, in going into situations that are challenging, we go not just as an isolated and powerless human being, but rather as one connected to 'the grid of being' in an invisible way. When we have inner spiritual assurance, it radiates out, making a difference to our lives and then other people pick up our sense of assurance intuitively. Then our power has returned and our light is on.

33

The Answers have Changed

The year 2020 was a time of massive change and dislocation due to the Covid-19 pandemic. It took a while for the symptoms of this silent plague to manifest, so we didn't know immediately if we were infected.

During the Spanish Flu of 1918 there was very little understanding of what caused the flu, and it spread rapidly. Viruses were only discovered in 1935 and were seen for the first time using an electron microscope in 1940. Eighty years later, during the 2020 Covid pandemic, we could see vastly enlarged graphic pictures of what the virus looked like while watching the news on TV. We then had a better understanding of what was happening and were able to take preventative measures.

It took scientists two weeks to sequence the Covid-19 virus in a lab and develop a test method to identify it. This represented a major breakthrough in our understanding of disease. No longer was God getting the blame for a pandemic, as happened in times past. Science now understands what the virus is and how it is spreading, although there were many who disputed the scientific interpretation.

There is a story about Albert Einstein when he lectured students in the 1930s. After lecturing he gave the students a test. A year later he did more lecturing to the same students and then gave the students another test. An assistant pointed out that the second test was the same one that Einstein had given the year before. To which Einstein answered, "The questions are the same, but the answers have changed."[59] At that time the study of physics was developing so rapidly that the understanding of the core concepts of physics was changing.

Some of the most important philosophical questions people have asked throughout history include:
- What is the truth?
- How do I experience love?
- How do I live my life?
- What is the cause of death?

In this post-modern era the answers to these fundamental questions are also changing.

When considering these questions, it is worth noting that we are now connected in ways that were never imagined. We have easy access to enlightened thinking that helps us become free from dogma and superstition. We have more access to information and advice on how to be loving, how to live longer and be healthier, than has ever been the case in the past. Access to this abundant information is cheaper than it has ever been; it is almost free.

It is a lousy life if we are living in a lazy, deceptive and untruthful way. To be aligned with spirit requires commitment, honesty and integrity. Then no matter what we have to face in our lives, we can deal with what comes along in a way that is inspired.

We need to recognize that the answers have changed. How we view our lives, our relationships and even our understanding of the truth is changing. It is important to have an ongoing enquiry into the truth, so as to integrate our lives with the experience of divinity. When living with a spiritual orientation in the background, we are able to bring that inspiration and insight into the circumstance that we find ourselves in, and new answers emerge.

34

A Gigantic Experiment

Human beings are social animals, who throughout the centuries have mostly been part of a community or tribe. In the year 2000 with the Covid-19 pandemic, in many countries where a lockdown was imposed, people were part of a gigantic experiment to stop a virus spreading, in a way that has never been tried before. Throughout history it has been the sick who were isolated; but for Covid-19 it was the general populace who were isolating or social distancing by law, so as not to succumb to the virus.

We all had to learn from this dramatic change in routine. It also gave me time to consider the spiritual lessons that can be learned from the lockdown. If we want to improve our lives spiritually, we can also experiment by trying new approaches on how to be more connected, how to live life fully and develop and enhance loving relationships even when isolated and distanced.

I find my life is an ongoing experiment as I continue to learn and grow through a process of spiritual discovery. But even during these experiments there will also be times when things don't work out as envisioned. Experimentation in exploring spiritual understanding needs to continue even when it seems boring, as it requires application to keep moving forward.

Part of the experimentation is discovering what it is to be part of a field; what Rupert Sheldrake[60] described as a morphic field where resonance is shared. When we are part of a morphic field we allow the flow to happen between us so that it also nourishes our soul, making us feel more alive at the core of ourselves.

To live a worthwhile life, it is essential that we serve others and not only ourselves. We can also provide a service at the soul level through sharing nourishing spiritual essences. The soul needs spiritual nourishment; it is not designed to be isolated. In the past we may have had adverse life experiences, but the healing occurs when the soul is nourished and inspired, as part of a field of collective spiritual resonance.

The spiritual lesson was to discover how to be in the world with a spiritually nourished soul regardless of any disaster. There are times when I've been so involved in my life that I have forgotten that I have an inner spiritual essence that needs nourishing. In a time of adverse circumstances when the old routine is broken it is very easy to slip into survival mode, rather than engaging in an essential service for the soul. But we can all be here to see beyond self-preoccupation and to conduct an ongoing experiment in seeing our lives as an opportunity for spiritual service as we bring enlightenment into the world.

35

Practice Thinking

Do we consciously practice the activity of thinking? In any field of activity, if one wants to improve, one has to practice. This is the case in sport, music, academics or any other field in which one wants to develop. Practice enhances our ability to undertake an activity. As we actively practice thinking it will make us better at it.

It is said that our thinking is often on automatic pilot. There are times when we are quite willing for this to be the case, when we are doing routine work, being entertained, playing or watching games. We all at times just need to switch off and relax. In this era, we have far more entertainment on screens than could ever have been imagined, which gives us an excuse not to engage in thinking.

What are we doing with our mind the rest of the time when we are not being entertained, playing games or watching screens? The question we can ask ourselves is, "Are we spending some of our time thinking in a way that is interesting, disciplined and creative?" To be creative may need disciplined application. Creativity also requires a willingness to go in new directions; it is a process of trial and error in considering new ways of seeing and doing things, which includes initiating new thinking in an area under consideration.

There is a movie about the life of the American pop artist *Roy Lichtenstein*[61] who experimented for many years to develop his creative style before receiving acclaim as an artist at the age of 38. He had been copying other artists' styles, but to be successful he had to think how to express his creations on canvas in an original way.

Many people suffer from boredom. But if you are bored it's time to read, explore new ideas and think in a creative way, rather than recycling old thoughts or switching off and thinking of nothing. People often get stuck in a closed loop of thinking. It takes some application to think in an original way that initiates something new. It is the kind of thinking that allows fresh ideas to emerge.

We can consider whether there is inertia or mental lethargy in our thinking, and to what degree we engage in second-hand thinking. Second-hand thinking is a regurgitation of old, unoriginal ideas without any analysis or perspective.

Thinking original thoughts doesn't magically happen. It takes application, contemplation and consideration and also reading, watching talks, podcasts and motivational material. We may also have to devote some time in our day to contemplating and considering something new. In thinking fresh thoughts, we are taking what we already know and then thinking into the unknown.

Thinking doesn't come out of a vacuum; it develops from what has previously been thought and written down by others. In thinking with an open mind, we can then add a new perspective, insight and understanding. We can initiate a new direction and build and develop on what we already know.

We may find that a thinking approach we already have may work well for a period of time, until it becomes stale or our life changes. Then we have to re-imagine, rethink and rediscover a new way of thinking and doing. That propels us forward and gets us out of the mental lethargy and the spiritual inertia of second-hand thinking. We then can break out of an enclosed loop of thinking and find a new way to go forward.

It is also important not to think in an isolated way, but rather to find ways of engaging and motivating people around us, so that we create collective momentum. To generate momentum in a group can at times be a big challenge to undertake. How do we motivate ourselves and others to keep moving forward while society is static and locked into an old way of thinking? Forward propulsion doesn't happen automatically; we have to engage at all levels with other people so that we gain their interest and buy-in.

The process creating forward propulsion includes dealing with problems, issues and ideas as they arise, engaging in open conversation and collaborative consideration. It is finding creative solutions while in the background developing trust.

There are many people who don't want to think at all and are content to just follow instructions and perform tasks in a mechanical way. But there is more enjoyment in finding new ways of thinking and expressing. Initiating a change in thinking is not easy, but it improves our life when we do so.

36

Exposing Negatives

I have previously referred to the expression, 'having a Kodak moment', which is taking a picture at a particular moment to remember for posterity. A future generation of kids may not even know what the word 'Kodak' means. Eastman Kodak was a corporation that pioneered photography, then went bankrupt in 2012. Previously, it was one of the largest corporations in the world and it looked like it would last forever, but only a remnant of the company has survived and most of its photography products have disappeared.

The reason why Kodak went bankrupt was that despite having invented digital photography, it did not immediately implement that invention. At the time, Kodak made most of their money out of processing film, so they stayed with film. When other companies developed digital photography, Kodak got left behind.[62] Now almost all photography is digital.

Taking pictures with our phones has largely replaced using cameras. When the change to digital photography happened, Kodak did not adapt to the change. So now we can say that 'having a Kodak moment' means seeing a future trend, but not adapting to the change!

Circumstances change in all our lives, and we need to adapt to the new future as it unfolds. Camera film gave us a limited number of pictures per roll of film and after the pictures were taken the spool was sent away for processing in a darkroom, where the negatives were converted into positives, which were called photographs. The spool was first chemically treated and then a light was shone through the negative to produce an enlarged positive picture on light-sensitive photographic paper. When the negatives got exposed to the light, a positive was created by shining a light through the negative.

We also can shine a light on the negatives we may hold in consciousness! Psychologically, we may have negatives about ourselves and about other people. The processing of photographic negatives is done in the dark. But if you process the negatives for too long in the dark, they become overexposed and begin to fade. It is important to have an honest look at one's life and acknowledge what negatives exist and then transform them into positives through enlightenment, so one can move forward. Otherwise, the negatives remain negative and become a limiting factor in the background of our life.

By having an honest look at oneself, the negatives one is harboring can be transformed with the aid of compassion. This includes having compassion for one's own negatives and the negatives in a relationship with another person. After 31 years of marriage (at the time of writing) I know that one cannot have a long-term relationship where there are no negatives.

But one can have compassion for the negatives that are there, rather than arguing, trying to prove you are right, or getting angry or frustrated.

Dealing with the negatives with compassion is a process of letting go with patience and understanding, as one accepts any shortcomings with an enlightened perspective. Transforming the negatives into positives includes engaging in conversation so that a new picture of the relationship can emerge. Stuck with the negatives is not a good place to stay. If we see with perspective and have an openness to learn, we can change a conversation about the negatives, and create a new picture that will be sustained in the light.

We all have a picture of what our life is about, and we live into the picture that we have created. We can engage in creative conversation that does not ignore the negatives by pretending they are not there, but rather we can transform those negatives into a more positive picture.

37

The Wisdom of Monkeys

A friend of mine sent me a video clip of a young girl who asked her mother, "Where did we come from?" The mother replied, "We were created by God." Then the girl went and asked her father the same question. He replied, "Due to evolution over millions of years, we evolved from monkeys."

The little girl was confused by these two answers, so she got both parents together: "Dad says we evolved from monkeys and Mom says we were created by God," to which her mother quickly answered, "Your father's side of the family evolved from monkeys, but my side of the family was created by God." This is not a debate about creation versus evolution, but I came across an interesting quote from a website, Monkeyworlds.com: "Experts are in awe over the social attributes of monkey groups. The primates are very in tune with each other and what is going on around them. They often help each other with finding food, caring for the young and staying protected."[63]

Most people think that we can't learn anything from monkeys, other than observing them through the study of zoology.

We may also think we are vastly superior to monkeys in that we can:

- rationally think and make decisions
- imagine the future
- analyse the past and
- improve, using the scientific method.

But there's one thing that the monkeys may have developed more than most human beings: A natural wisdom that makes them in tune with each other and with what is going on around them.

We have to get back in tune with ourselves so that we can be more in tune with other people and in tune with spirit. In the modern world it is easy to get busy and race around trying to achieve, so that we find ourselves out of tune and experiencing a loss of power. When one is out of tune, one's relationships suffer, and one becomes oblivious to the environment.

There is another monkey that we must deal with; one that comes at great cost. This is the monkey that Tim Urban spoke about in a TED Talk in 2016,[64] which is the little monkey that we have inside ourselves called the 'instant gratification monkey'. In seeking immediate gratification, we do things that lack wisdom and understanding, that are irrational and self-destructive.

Through instant gratification we may sacrifice:
- our future
- our ability to be creative
- our ability to complete projects or get anything done
- our caring towards other people
  ... because, we are so ruled by that monkey inside us.

Often in seeking instant gratification we:
- don't do what we should do
- don't connect with others
- don't express care
- don't do things that enhance community
- don't do the things that uplift our spirit.

We have to fight our need for instant gratification, which may take the form of substance abuse, alcohol, sex, playing computer games, binge watching TV or just doing nothing, losing our energy and zoning out. Instead, we must find ways to be more spiritually and creatively engaged.

We can take more time to reflect, when we are no longer driven to be socially busy. There comes a time to stop socializing, attending events, parties and just going out for no reason, because staying home seems desolate. This can be a time for wisdom, for considering how to be of service and to find one's spiritual authenticity.

Trevor Noah, as host of *The Daily Show*, had a conversation with actor and British comedian Ricky Gervais. Gervais said: "Some things are more important than being smart and clever, like being kind."[65] I thought this was particularly interesting coming from Ricky Gervais who specializes in nasty and cringe-worthy comments in his humor. It's a breakthrough that he now realizes the importance of being kind.

It's good to think about being kind to the people who we come into contact with daily. Even the monkeys have figured out the importance of being kind to each other!

38

The Spiritual Terrain

Louis Pasteur said, when approaching his death, "Le microbe n'est rien, le 'terrain' est tout." Translated into English: "The microbe is nothing, the 'terrain' is everything."[66] Pasteur was the father of the Germ Theory of Disease, which is still the dominant theory in medicine today, yet this statement is at odds with that theory.

In 19th century France, while Pasteur was advocating the notion of germs as the cause of disease, another French scientist named Antoine Béchamp was developing *terrain* theory. Béchamp advocated not destroying germs, but the cultivation of health through diet, hygiene and healthy lifestyle practices, such as breathing fresh air and taking regular exercise.[67] Clearly this theory also applies to maintaining health, in that good diet and an active lifestyle leads to greater health and vitality and increases the body's ability to fight germs and viruses.

The idea is that if the person has a strong immune system (or 'terrain' as Béchamp called it), then germs will not multiply and overwhelm the body's good health. In 'terrain' theory, when health starts to decline due to personal neglect and poor lifestyle choices, then individuals are susceptible to infection. According to this approach, as the person restores health through diet, hygiene and detoxification, the infection goes away on its own. Béchamp's approach has been largely forgotten by the medical community, which is more focused on fighting germs and viruses.

I know a man who buys a two-liter bottle of sugary cola soda for lunch and then wonders why he has a weight problem and high blood sugar levels. The drink provides a temporary energy boost, but it actually destroys the terrain of his body. During the period of the Covid-19 pandemic, daily statistics indicated that among people infected with the virus, old age and co-morbidities were a major factor in causing death, while younger individuals who were active, fit and had a healthy lifestyle had a much higher rate of recovery without hospitalization.

This way of thinking about the 'terrain' does not only apply to infection, but also make a difference in uplifting our health mentally and spiritually. There are steps we can take to have a more vibrant mental and spiritual terrain. When facing difficulty, the question to consider is not *Why is this happening?* Rather to ask oneself, *What can I do at the mental and spiritual levels to change the terrain?*

There are small things we can do to uplift our spiritual terrain. It requires the right mental habits and an attitude more open to other ways of thinking. Often, when people face change or difficult circumstances, bad mental habits resurface. They may think how unfair or difficult a situation is and may see themselves as victims. Good mental and spiritual habits help us to accept what we are dealing with, so that we can then take positive steps forward. This includes an inquiring attitude and an interest in personal growth. We can then uplift ourselves through maintaining our personal atmosphere. Through spiritual attunement we can transform our mood.

The great Sufi mystic poet Rumi said: "Yesterday I was clever so I wanted to change the world. Today I am wise so I am changing myself."[68] Changing the spiritual terrain involves making ourselves more spiritually open and authentic. In a difficult situation, instead of giving up and surrendering to the situation in a defeatist way, we can surrender in way that leads to a greater self-awareness. In caring for our spiritual terrain, we uplift our circumstances and create a very different 'terrain' in which to live.

39

Invisible Wealth

_____

Paul Simon began writing songs in his teenage years. He performed his first song, 'The Girl for Me', with Art Garfunkel, when they were at school together. Simon was 16 when he published this song, which is impressive on its own.[69]

Simon continued to write and perform while keeping ownership of the intellectual property of his music. Simon retained ownership throughout his career, finally selling the rights to Sony Music Publishing for $250 million in March 2021.[70]

The songs appreciated in value and generated substantial royalties. The true value of a song is not based on the cost of how the lyrics and sheet music were initially created, performed and recorded, as many songs are recorded and are then soon forgotten. The value is determined by how often the song continues to be played and how famous the composer becomes.

Paul Simon won three Grammy Awards for 'Bridge over Troubled Waters', which was the #1 song on the Billboard 100 charts for 14 weeks in 1970.[71] It is a song that many of the 'baby boom' generation remember. The years 2019 and 2020 were times of 'troubled waters'; in 2019 there was global unrest, which was then followed by the Covid-19 pandemic that swept across the world in 2020.

Prior to the pandemic there was a feeling of injustice based on a cumulative build-up of racism and inequality. Then the pandemic confined most of the population to their homes causing a different type of distress. In the rapid change that came about during these events, normality broke down and it required wisdom to navigate through the uncertainty.

Invisible Wealth, a book of essays by leading economists, compiled by Arnold Kling and Nick Schultz,[72] is about that which is invisible but has value, such as education, the rule of law, property rights and innovation. These are factors that cannot readily be seen but make a substantial difference in generating wealth in a community or country.

We often ignore the invisible aspects of our lives, not seeing the impact they have. Then we feel hard done by, because our lives are not up to the standard we had hoped for.

There is also an invisible quality of atmosphere and

radiance that can be described as 'spiritual enlightenment', which is a result of the generation of *'spiritual wealth'*. Generating *spiritual wealth* is a life-long, continuous learning process. *Spiritual wealth* implies having an in-depth experience of divinity and knowing spiritual resonance, rather than just observing and repeating ritual or relying on belief.

As we generate *spiritual wealth* we enlighten and uplift ourselves and have a finer quality of life. The factors that generate spiritual enlightenment are:

- Enquiry and interest
- Spiritual education
- Spiritual authenticity
- Resonating with divinity.

These four factors lead to the generation of spiritual growth that is real, authentic and in tune. As one walks along the path towards spiritual maturity, we have to grow up, spiritually speaking. It is not always an easy thing to do as there will be challenges along the way.

It is important not to fall into the trap of self-righteousness; that is, saying to yourself that your beliefs are right and the beliefs that others have are wrong, and then not engaging in enquiry, interest, or having an openness to an ongoing consideration.

When we have walked a spiritual path, we can deal with what comes our way because we have an invisible base on which to stand. It is not just formed by a belief system; rather, it is something known at the core of ourselves that brings stability and inner assurance into the rest of our lives.

Whatever circumstances we find ourselves in, even if we are doing routine things like going shopping or doing chores, we can still be spiritually consistent and remember that we have an invisible quality to our lives that makes a difference. As we take care of the invisible aspect of ourselves, we are at peace. There is a sense of knowing, and we no longer feel fragile when dealing with troubled waters. By taking care of our *spiritual wealth*, we feel reassured and blessed.

40

The Bridge of Love

I enjoy traveling through the Tsitsikamma National Park, which is an 80 km drive down the N2 national route on the east coast of South Africa. Along the way the road travels over the Storms River bridge and the Bloukrans River bridge (a famous bungee jumping station) which span two large ravines. The views are panoramic.

Rumi said: "Love is the bridge between you and everything."[73] It takes some strength of character and commitment to build bridges of love. I know that in marriage or any long-term relationship, to live closely with someone in a creative relationship is to be continually building the bridge of love, while managing daily activities and challenges, as circumstances change over time.

There are five characteristics we need to remember to sustain any loving relationship, namely:

- **Patience**: Anyone who has been in a relationship for a long period of time will have had their patience tested.
- **Consistency**: There is value in acting in a consistent manner even when the outcome is not clear.
- **Understanding**: Strive to understand the other person's motives and actions and why they think what they think and do what they do.
- **Trust**: To be trustworthy strengthens a relationship.
- **Forgiveness**: There will be times when one has to forgive, or one wants to be forgiven.

These five attributes build a relationship of love. It is essential to avoid arrogance or insist on always having things done 'my way' without ever considering the other person's feelings, ideas or vision. Rather, the relationship gets stronger when each side learns to be flexible and accommodating while still maintaining standards and not sacrificing fundamental values.

Building a bridge to the future takes:

- **Listening**: At times we are required to speak, but most of the time what is required in relationships is listening. Listening builds bridges with other people.

- **Innovation**: Life becomes boring if one does not venture out or try new things. We have to experiment and find out what works; take on new challenges and find new opportunities. There is no limit to what we can innovate.
- **Adaptability**: To be willing to change and adapt to circumstances as they present themselves. It is failure to adapt that leads to people missing the opportunity to go forward in a creative way.

When one is feeling down or has a wounded heart, the key thing is to remember one's invisible connection in the relationship. We may also need to treat past relationships as water under the bridge and move on. We have to let go of what happened in the past and not get stuck with what was not generative. Sometimes the loving thing to do is to let go or walk away. As we move on and get back into the flow, we will find new opportunities to share our love.

41

Internal Tone

The National Arts Festival is held at Makanda in the Eastern Cape of South Africa (formerly called Grahamstown, home of Rhodes University). In 2020, Peter Martens from Stellenbosch University played the Bach Cello Suite, # 3 in C Major. Listening to the cello was magnificent; its rich quality of tone is so appealing as the strings vibrate in a pattern of resonance. I listened to this concert over the internet, and still was able to tune in to Martens' fine quality of playing. Consider that people can also experience resonance when they spend time together, or when they connect over the internet, if the quality of tone is uplifting.

The cello has 12 chord types; the musician has to play all the notes that make the chord, and each note must be in tune with the other. In our life, one of the better experiences we have is when we are in accord and resonant with other people in an inspiring way.

That lifts us out of a bland or boring experience. By contrast, when listening to a news bulletin on radio or TV, there will be reports of discord in the world. Experts discuss these situations and share theories about the causes of the discord, but they seldom offer a solution outside of the accepted political views but that is unlikely to transform the discord into accord.

In music there can be discordant notes which are then resolved into harmony in a way that is pleasing to listen to. Likewise in our lives, when our internal experience is discordant, it is good to resolve discord back into accord. It is the experience of accord at the core of ourselves that stabilizes our mental and emotional state. In becoming aware of the effect that our internal tone has, we become more interested in resolving an experience of inner discord so as to uplift our lives.

If we are out of tune internally, we can retune ourselves to experience a finer tone which will then permeate our thinking and our emotional state. One of the qualities of a spiritually mature person is knowing when to come back into accord. Feelings of discouragement or disillusionment can be caused by a state of inner discord. What is needed then is to transform that inner state. Inner accord may not seem that important, but it makes a significant difference in our lives; it determines how much we enjoy ourselves and how empowered we feel.

Consider how much violence is caused by people's inner discord which is then acted out. Once people experience discord internally, they lash out because they don't have an ability to resolve issues. It is useful to be able to resolve discord with other people before the situation deteriorates.

Leading management consultant Peter Drucker once said: "The best way to predict the future is to create it."[74] So, we are either creating a future in accord or out of a state of discord. To create our future, we have to ask what we are in accord with, and what we can bring to a situation that will create harmony. Peter Drucker also said: "The most important thing in communication is to hear what isn't being said."[75] That requires us to develop an intuitive sense of hearing that is beyond the spoken word. Sometimes, what isn't openly expressed is love, understanding or appreciation, even when it is known intuitively. Similarly, when negative energy is unexpressed, people feel that they are invalidated, disrespected, undermined or misunderstood.

A vibrant culture of sharing, listening and love assists us to create our future. We play a role in establishing the culture in which our future is created. As we set the tone internally for our future, what emerges will be of finer quality.

42

Going Deep

Having a wide range of different experiences will not compensate for living a shallow life. When we have a commitment to develop a depth of understanding, our life will be more inspiring and uplifted. In having an in-depth experience one can then also share that greater range with other people who are also interested in having a deeper, more meaningful experience.

There are some people who, after a spiritual experience over a weekend or having read a book, think they know it all. They may soon forget some of what they have learned or never apply it. As we maintain our spiritual inquiry over a period of time it will build, so that we then have a more vibrant spiritual experience. It is not a matter of just acquiring spiritual knowledge; the teaching must go further so that it actually influences our life.

Spiritual knowledge is essential to create a foundation on which to build. There are also a few who have studied widely, but their depth of experience and understanding is superficial.

Ongoing spiritual commitment generates a spiritual atmosphere that is authentic. It takes awareness and practice to consciously generate and sustain a spiritual atmosphere. We have to understand that the atmosphere we generate has an influence on our own life and on the lives of other people we come into contact with.

Rather than living a superficial life, we may increase our self-awareness by asking ourselves:

- *Why is this so?*
- *Can I go deeper?*
- *What in my outlook needs to change?*

It takes self-enquiry and depth to be aware of the atmosphere that we generate.

When we become spiritually self-aware it changes our lives as we are operating at another level. It transforms the quality of the environment in which we live and it adds a dimension to our lives that wasn't there before. As we transform our inner vibration to be more spiritually in tune, we feel integrated and blessed. It changes the quality of our relationships and friendships.

Whatever circumstance and situation we find ourselves in, even if there is a general lack of order, attempting to dominate and impose our will does not make the environment peaceful. Rather, it takes a change in atmosphere that is conducive to more creative relationships and more creative solutions. As there is a consciousness of a shared higher quality of atmosphere the possibility for resolution opens up.

43

Kindness and Reciprocity

There is a book called *Humankind: A Hopeful History* by Dutch historian Rutger Bregman.[76] In considering the word humankind, it should be remembered that it includes the word *kind*. It is Bregman's view that, throughout history, human kindness has made a big difference in the lives of humanity and helped civilizations progress.

In his book Bregman differs with a view held by some psychologists and philosophers, that human beings are by nature selfish and governed by self-interest. A review in *The Times* newspaper[77] points out that "he has written a book that is filled with tales of human goodness." Bregman maintains that "we are hardwired for kindness, geared toward co-operation rather than competition and are more inclined to trust rather than distrust one another."[78]

There is also a history of human nastiness, as people seek to dominate and invalidate others. It includes what happened through wars and slavery. We may have also experienced nastiness in our lives or watched nastiness perpetrated in violent movies and on TV.

Nastiness is destructive, wrecking relationships of all kinds, whereas kindness creates relationship and generates trust. We all have to consider when it is better to be kind rather than right in a friendship or relationship. Sometimes it is better to give up a self-righteous view and be kind because it leads to a better outcome.

Bregman's book also offers a very different view of history from what I was taught at school. When I studied history, we learned about the wars that countries fought, where the victorious generals and fighters were idolized. We didn't learn a history of kindness or about good deeds to help others, which may not be as interesting or dramatic. Yet, according to Bregman, a history of kindness exists. Instead of being purely competitive, it is in our nature and best interests to be kind and cooperative. People also prefer to trust rather than distrust. Human beings have cooperated and built trust throughout history, which has helped them progress. History has shown that humans have learned to get on with other people and resolve conflict, so as to live in peace and thrive.

Expressing kindness makes a positive difference in

our life and in the lives of others. But it is not just a matter of being kind in a naive way, so that we are easily exploited due to a lack of wisdom about people's motives. Rather, we need to consider kindness in the context of *reciprocity*. The dictionary.com[79] website's definition for reciprocity is 'exchanging for mutual benefit'.

This doesn't fully describe it in my view.[80] Rather, reciprocity is sharing in a generative way at the physical, mental, emotional and spiritual levels. It isn't just an exchange at the physical level for mutual benefit. There is a joy that comes when there is a depth of sharing at the mental and emotional level in an intimate way, creating a shared understanding through the flow of ideas built on trust and acceptance. It is important for humanity to thrive through having reciprocal relationships that nourish the soul and that foster the quality of love.

In the song, 'Nature Boy', sung by Nat King Cole, there are these words: "The greatest thing you'll ever learn is just to love and be loved in return."[81] Love has to be reciprocal if it is going to mean anything. There is vastly more value in a reciprocal relationship than in an exploitative one. When we choose to *love and be loved in return*, rather than being right, winning the argument or scoring points, it makes a significant difference in the quality of our lives. It is one of the most important choices we can make.

We may share ideas, thoughts, views and friendship, but there is also an energetic interchange behind what is said that elevates what is shared. There is an inspiring spiritual quality to reciprocation.

Reciprocation is essential for spiritual education. It is not a matter of *getting* a spiritual education in a theoretical way; rather, in the process of spiritual education there has to be a *giving and receiving* so that a flow is experienced that enlightens the soul.

In spiritual education, learning spiritual principles or being inspired by a teacher provides a foundation on which to build.

Without a teacher progress will be slow. To elevate spiritual education requires active engagement and response so as to experience reciprocal flow. To have a spiritual experience requires expressing what has been learned, showing engagement and participation. If nothing is expressed in return, the flow becomes stagnant, and it becomes difficult to continue to experience and understand with greater depth.

There are many ways to engage spiritually: through verbal expression, in writing, or through serving by doing duties and helping out with a caring attitude. Over and above what is taught in lectures, we learn when we take action, express ourselves and apply what we have learnt. It takes spiritual application built on understanding to have a truly profound experience.

In March 2017 Pope François wrote, "Rivers do not drink their own water; trees do not eat their own fruit; the sun does not shine on itself ... Living for others is a rule of nature. We are all born to help each other. Life is ... much better when others are happy because of you."[82] The way nature works is that each living organism isn't an isolated entity, but rather there are reciprocal relationships between plants and animals throughout nature. Biological research has discovered ecological systems that function through reciprocity.

In our lives it is wiser to interact with reciprocity, by being conscious of having an energetic interchange that is generative, rather than acting is a way that is extractive. Then we can deal with whatever comes along in a way that is life-enhancing.

44

Courage and Intentions

———————————

Ronald Reagan was quoted as saying "many a man has failed because he had a wishbone where his backbone should have been". This quote was used in a newsletter published in 2019 by John Steenhuisen, leader of the Democratic Alliance in South Africa. Steenhuisen went on to write, "If our economy – and indeed our country – could be built on wishes and intentions alone, we'd be unstoppable... But when it comes to turning those promises into reality we are always left wanting."[83]

This applies in our lives; in that we may promise ourselves that we will make a change, but we don't always follow through. We may have a vision of ourselves as implementing an immortality project to make a change in world, but it takes some backbone to continue to do the work and make a difference. Making a difference is a far better alternative to living an empty meaningless existence, where some individuals survive by using drugs and alcohol. It is also going to take courage and persistence to contemplate and consider our life and then be open to change, to create a life with more meaning. It is worthless pretending to change to boost our ego and make ourselves feel important, while continuing to be stuck in old ways of thinking.

It is not easy or comfortable to make a change. It takes courage to be honest enough to admit to oneself that there is a need for change, and then follow through with persistence so as to live in tune with one's soul. We will find that uplifting our consciousness brings change to our lives. That change then spreads out wider than our own small life, as other people come into the equation and new avenues and possibilities open.

45

Ripples of Hope

On 4 June 2016, the University of Cape Town (UCT) honored the 50th anniversary of Robert Kennedy's famous 'Ripples of Hope' speech.[84] The event was hosted by Robert Kennedy's daughter, Kerry Kennedy and the Kennedy family, together with UCT Chancellor Graça Machel, widow of Nelson Mandela. It was an event that highlighted South Africa's ongoing struggle for social justice.

The 'Ripples of Hope' speech is regarded as one of Robert Kennedy's finest. He said, "But each of us can act to change a small portion of events ... Each time a man stands up for an ideal or acts to improve the lot of others, or strikes out against injustice, he sends forth a tiny ripple of hope ... those ripples build a current."[85]

Are we aware of what ripples we are sending out? Do we send out ripples of hope that are spiritually uplifting and inspiring? To be sending out spiritual ripples of hope we need to be mindful of what we are expressing. We need to be aware of the mental habits that we have and the impulses that distract us. To also be aware of those elements that may impede our capacity to have a positive spiritual influence on the events that shape our lives.

To emanate a finer quality of spirit implies that we discover what is sacred at the core of ourselves. When our inner state is governed by feelings of anxiety, fear or sadness, instead of living in tune with the finer qualities of our soul, that then ripples out. To change those negative feelings, find something uplifting to read or listen to, or find someone who is expressing a more inspiring message that one can tune into.

This event was also attended by US Rep. John Lewis, a highly regarded Civil Rights activist in the 1960s who passed away on 17 July 2020. In his speech at the event, Lewis spoke about "a good kind of trouble that young people need to embrace."[86] We need to ask ourselves what kind of trouble we embrace; people often embrace the bad kind; that is, taking risks that lead to harm rather than growth.

There are those who assist 'youth at risk', like Pastor Craven Engle of the First Community Resource Centre, Hanover Park, Cape Town. They work to improve the lives of individuals who have embraced 'bad trouble' in gang infested neighborhoods. We are considering embracing the good kind of trouble that sends 'ripples of hope' outward, leading to creative opportunity. That is, taking risks to uplift our lives and our community in a positive way.

Ironically, while John Lewis was speaking, a group of protesters appeared and stood in front of him with placards denouncing high student fees, American imperialism and other issues. Lewis continued to deliver his message despite the protest. He stayed on message rather than reacting to the intrusion. At the time of speaking, he didn't lose his focus and the protesters were acknowledged later on. There will be times when, regardless of what is going on right in front of us, it is better to stay on message and continue to send out ripples of hope.

In sending out ripples of hope we must be aware of our network. In network theory, according to Metcalfe's Law,[87] *the value of the network increases exponentially according to the number of nodes in the network.*[88] We are all connected to other people through family, friends, associates and colleagues, but what is the quality of those connections? Do we bring ripples of spiritual hope to our network?

The networks that we have, whether at work or in our personal lives with our family or friends, connect us with other people and contextualize our lives.

If there is a finer spiritual quality at the core of ourselves, we naturally express ripples of hope into that network. As we are spiritually lit up and alive, we send ripples of hope to others.

46

Objective Truth

Scientist Neil deGrasse Tyson once said, "A great challenge of life: Knowing enough to think you are right, but not knowing enough to know you are wrong."[89] He says, "The good thing about Science is that it's true whether or not you believe in it."[90] The scientific truth that Neil deGrasse Tyson describes is an objective truth where everything is measurable, quantifiable and can easily be replicated under the same conditions. But research can emerge that eclipses the accepted scientific view. Over a period of time even scientists have to change their theories based on new evidence. For example, some of the theories of gravity by the great scientist Isaac Newton were overtaken by theories by Einstein. This was proved in an experiment by astronomers Dyson and Eddington in 1919[91] when they observed an eclipse. They proved that the accepted scientific truth about gravity had changed.

We may have an opinion and think we are right, and then get into a fight to show how right we are! Rather than be locked into a polarization of right and wrong; it is good to consider whether we know enough, have a grasp of all the underlying factors or have a depth of understanding.

Finding one's truth is more than just subscribing to a set of beliefs. It goes beyond agreeing with ideology or politics. We may encounter people who won't consider an alternative view if it interferes with their existing perspective of what they think the truth is. To defend their view; they may use the tactic of having a domineering personality or they may also have a lack of conscience or have no moral sense of right and wrong. To be aligned with truth takes courage. There may be a time where it is necessary to take a stand so as to protect family and friends, projects, career, business and community.

Philosophic or spiritual truth cannot be quantified. It is a truth that is life enhancing and includes how interconnected and interdependent we are. It is a truth that transforms our lives, and it is able to adapt to emerging change. It is not just a conceptual truth, but rather a truth that is expansive and strengthening.

There is an inner peace that radiates out when aligned with spiritual truth that is in tune with our soul. For us to be at peace comes from the atmosphere that we generate, when we align our inner state with philosophic and spiritual truth.

47

Vibrating Energy

The book *You*, by Charles F Haanel, says the following: "As the quality and value of all forms of energy are due to their rates of vibration, it follows that color will indicate the quality of the vibrating energy."[92] As we see color, we are seeing the spectrum of vibration that the colors are made up of.

Haanel also wrote "Everything in the universe vibrates...yes, everything". All force, all matter, all energy – even your life itself – is then a vibratory activity that conforms to precise natural laws.

So if you really want to understand why the universe is the way it is, you must come to an understanding of how vibrations operate and manifest. At school, I saw an experiment of light refracting through a glass prism. Through refraction, the different light waves are split into the seven colors of the rainbow.

Dutch astronomer, W Snell van Royen, discovered in 1621 the science of refraction, which is the wave nature of light, known as Snell's Law.[93] This discovery was subsequently developed by Descartes and Fermat. As light refracts into seven colors when passing through a prism, each color has its own vibrational signature. In fact, we live in a world that is filled with vibrating energy, that we see as color.

Human beings also carry vibrational energy that reflects what they are attuned to. It requires self-awareness to understand this. If one is attuned to the lowest level of vibration, life will be a struggle and will manifest in a mean, nasty or violent way. In a bizarre way, behavior that is awful, mean and nasty, is acted out by people who try to control others by acting in a dominating or undermining way. People who commit cruel, aggressive acts are attuned to a low level of energy, rather than being attuned and resonant to a more harmonious state. Random acts of violence occur because people live dysfunctional lives and are not aware that they are out of tune with harmonious living.

As CEO of a manufacturing business in Cape Town, I decided that, due to a decline in public transport, we would take our staff home in pick-up trucks with a canopy on the back. At that time, there were protests and unrest that flared up in isolated pockets in cities around the country. These protests were not reported in the media, so we didn't know in advance if the truck was entering an area of unrest. Our truck went down a road where people were protesting. The protesters had no particular animosity against us but started stoning vehicles, including our truck. The windows were shattered, and the bodywork dented. The driver and passengers felt shaken and frightened though they were fortunately not hurt. We were concerned about them but they felt secure enough to come to work the next day.

In South Africa, we have insurance for special risks such as civil commotion, public disorder, strikes, riots and terrorism and so the pick-up truck was fixed. But we can't insure ourselves against the vibrational ugliness that people experience that may manifest in random violence.

To effect real change, look inside and awaken to the quality of your vibration, then transform that. Find a way at the core of yourself to express a vibration aligned with creative energy and abundance. Do this by associating with other people who carry that higher vibration. That is to find a way to be filled with light and love rather than darkness, fear and inadequacy. If one has a higher quality of vibration at the core of oneself, one is also able to express truth and know self-assurance.

People say, "I can't do that. I have this history, this past, these circumstances that were bad and therefore this justifies me thinking these inadequate and disempowering thoughts.".They may not say this so explicitly, but that may be what they feel. Blaming the past is not a justification for the present. If one examined one's personal history going back a few generations, most people would discover that their ancestors suffered or were treated badly by the rulers of the day. The more one researches it, the more one will find out about a history of famine, pestilence, disease, brutal wars and revolutions that caused suffering to almost all people around the world. Even in the Bible these stories are told.

No matter what is happening in our lives, we have *this moment,* and our challenge is how to deal creatively with what is happening now. Just blaming the past or feeling victimized is not a substitute for a creative and caring approach. There are many ways to be creative and adapt to current circumstances and solve problems in a vibrant way. We can add an artistic touch and bring color to what we do. We can be an artist, even in the most mundane and difficult circumstances. We can transform a situation, even when working in a warehouse, cooking a meal or cleaning a room.

Rather than throwing metaphorical stones – or real stones, as happened with my truck – all situations can be repaired and recreated as we shine the light, differentiate the vibration and bring a new range of spiritual color. We can be original and proactive rather than just reacting to what is going on by protesting and complaining. We have a unique opportunity to be attuned to a higher vibration in what we share together, so that we deal with what is happening in the world in a creative and original way.

48

Kunene and the King

In August 2020 one of South Africa's greatest actors, John Kani, celebrated his 77th birthday. In May 2019, I saw Kani at the Fugard Theatre in Cape Town, with Sir Anthony Sher, in a play called *Kunene and the King*. This play, written by Kani, was about two old men from different racial and economic backgrounds coping with change in their lives. The internet platform 'Scribd Inc.' had a review that said, "Kani's script captured the complex divides of race, class and politics in South Africa."[94]

Kani plays a black male nurse sent to look after a narcissistic, cantankerous actor (played by Sher) who is preparing to play King Lear, whilst suffering from cancer. As the play develops, they learn to cope with diminished expectations, understand their backgrounds and then reconcile with each other. In the play, it was inspiring to see these men overcome the suffering they had experienced.

John Kani previously featured in the *Black Panther* movie as T'Chaka, father and spiritual inspiration of the Marvel character, Black Panther. The role of Black Panther in the movie was played by Chadwick Boseman who died of colon cancer on 28 August 2020 at the young age of 43.

In an interview on local talk radio the day after Boseman's death, John Kani celebrated the life and mourned the passing of Chadwick Boseman. The two had remained friends after making the movie. He said that when they met, Chadwick greeted him in isiXhosa, the African language that Kani had spoken in the movie.

Chadwick had colon cancer while acting in some of his greatest movies in the four years before he died. He had struggled with his illness, yet he portrayed strength, inspiring people through the roles he played. Vice President Kamala Harris described Chadwick Boseman as, "brilliant, kind, learned and humble."[95] To be remembered in that way says a lot about the character of the man.

Chadwick Boseman once said in a valedictory speech: "Your very existence is wrapped up in the things you need to fulfill. The struggles along the way are only meant to shape you for your purpose."[96] This is an inspiring comment. He realized that despite his struggle he had a purpose to fulfill. Through his acting he inspired others.

Achievement through a career or business is one way to experience purpose, but there is also a need to fulfill spiritual purpose, by living an uplifting life and then radiating that out into the world. Part of fulfilling spiritual purpose is being a loving, caring, kind and humble person, as well as having other fine traits.

In awakening spiritually, we find that our lives take on a spiritual purpose. We become spiritual activists by activating our spiritual core. Activists are normally seen as protesting against something, dealing with issues and complaints about the status quo. Sometimes we have to have the courage to take a stand against injustice, but spiritual activists do not just promote a set of beliefs; rather, they choose to be spiritually active and alive. One of the themes in the *Black Panther* movie is overcoming adversity; T'Challa must find his spiritual core and purpose within the context of a Marvel universe.

What I am considering is that at the very core of ourselves, we can be spiritually active so that our expression is 'switched on' and carries an 'inner enlightenment'. When we are internally switched on, our expression has influence outwards and we live a life that has purpose and meaning.

When we are spiritually switched on, our energy

level changes for the better. We no longer act as a narcissistic, cantankerous person, but rather we are spiritually alive, no matter what constraints we face. People easily slip into a state of justified complaint and become an activist against something. Just being against something is not a good purpose to dedicate one's life to in the long term. A more rewarding purpose is to be active in creating an inner harmony and expressing that into the world.

There is a term in mathematics called Delta (Δ) which means change. As we change the inner tone to be more harmonious, we change the energy we experience. This can be described as an equation, Δ Tone = Δ Energy. This equation applies in our lives. As we take responsibility to be in harmony with our spiritual self, we feel more energized. We then live in resonant accord with others who carry a spiritually inspired vibration.

Acknowledgements

I would like to thank my wife Fiona who has been at my side and supported me when I initially shared these ideas. Fiona also assisted me greatly with the final edit.

I would like to thank my editor Cathy Eden who also did extensive editing and has assisted me in improving my writing style so as to better express my ideas.

I would like to thank Howard Goodman and Anne-Lise Bure Shepherd, from the Gatehouse Spiritual Centre, who have provided a platform through the Sunday Morning Meetings, which then I transcribed into this book.

I would like to thank David Karchere, the Spiritual Director of Sunrise Ranch, whose weekly post, 'The Pulse of Spirit', provided a starting point and inspiration for many of the themes under consideration.

About the Author

Laurence Gawronsky has an interest in philosophy and in developing spiritual insight. He is married to Fiona and has two sons in their 20's.

He manages his own business and lives in Cape Town, South Africa. He is active in hiking on the mountain, going to the beach and enjoys sport, movies and theater.

Endnotes

1. https://en.wikipedia.org/wiki/Waka_Waka_ (This_Time_for_Africa)

2. https://www.prnewswire.com/news-releases/ fifa-world-cup-2010-official-song-waka-waka- this-time-for-africa-becomes-global- phenomenon-98418234.html

3. https://www.collinsdictionary.com/ dictionary/ english/ecology

4. https://yellow.place/en/the-8-o-clock- clubcape- town-southafrica Notes made by author.

5. https://en.wikipedia.org/wiki/Irma_Stern

6. The Denial of Death by Ernest Becker (Author) Winner of the Pulitzer Prize in 1974

7. Congressman John Lewis remembers MLK 50 years later 3 Apr 2018 https://www.wusa9. com/article/news/history/martin-luther- king-50-years-later-congressman-john-lewis- remembers-his-legacy/65-534714765

8. https://en.wikipedia.org/wiki/Nephesh

9. Carl Schultz – BibleStudyTools.com https:// www.biblestudytools.com/dictionary/soul/

10. Carl Schultz – BibleStudyTools.com

11. Survival of the Friendliest Brian Hare and Vanessa Woods. Published by Random House Trade Paperbacks Jul 13, 2021

12. On the Origin of Species: Charles Darwin fifth edition (published in 1869)

13. https://www.britannica.com/topic/Jew- people

14. https://www.britannica.com/topic/Elohim

15. https://metaphysicist.com/problems/being/

16. Psalms 51:6 "Behold, You desire truth in the innermost Being". Proverbs 20:27 : The spirit of man is the lamp of the Lord. Serving all the innermost parts of being."

17. https://english.stackexchange.com/ questions/ 52589/when-was-the-word-being- first-used-to- refer-to-a-human-being-or- sentient-being

18. https://quoteinvestigator.com/2019/06/20/ spiritual/

19. https://www.theclearingnw.com/blog/ spiritual- beings-having-a-human-experience

20. https://en.wikipedia.org/wiki/Thomas_Paine

21. https://www.goodreads.com/quotes/889423- he- who-dares-not-offend-cannot-be- honesthttps:// www.goodreads.com/ quotes/889423-he-who- dares-not-offend- cannot-be-honest

22. https://www.washingtonpost. com/ graphics/ 2019/investigations/ afghanistanpapers/ afghanistan-war- confidentialdocuments/

23. https://www.vox. com/ 2019/12/30/21039298/40-celsius- australia- fires-2019-heatwave-climate-change

24. https://www.washingtonpost.com/ nation/ 2019/02/11/mass-invasion-polarbears- is- terrorizing-an-island-town-climatechange- is- blame/

25. https://images.app.goo.gl/ vNoYyMCpFED9UoG58

26. https://en.wikipedia.org/wiki/2019_United_ Nations_Climate_Change_Conference

27. https://www.forbes.com/sites/ emanuelabarbiroglio/2019/12/06/cop25greta- thunberg-arrives-in-madrid/

28. https://www.forbes.com/sites/ emanuelabarbiroglio/2019/12/06/cop25greta- thunberg-arrives-in-madrid/

29. https://climate.nasa.gov/ask- nasaclimate/2949/ why-milankovitch- orbitalcycles-cant-explain- earths-current- warming/

30. Progress: Ten Reasons to Look Forward to the Future: Johan Norberg, One World Publications https://www. simonandschuster.com/books/ Progress/ Johan-Norberg/9781786070654

31. https://www.howardstern.com/ show/ 2019/11/04/video-trevor-noah- revealswhy-he- cant-stop-working-how-he- learneddeal-anger- advice-dave-chappelle/

32. Spilich, G. J., Vesonder, G. T., Chiesi, H. L., & Voss, J. F. (1979). Text processing of domain- related information for individuals with high and low domain knowledge. Journal of Verbal Learning and Verbal Behavior, 18(3), 275-290

33. C. G.Jung Letters, Vol.1 1906 – 1950

34. Tony Robbins Crisis in Leadership Playbook

https://real-leaders.com/tony/6/

35. Smarter than you Think by Clive Thompson. William Collins Publishers, 2013.

36. https://www.theguardian.com/money/2018/nov/05/firms-switched-four-day-weekincrease-efficiency-health-happiness

37. http://www.bfmi.at/concert_yoyo_ma_in_athens_the_bach_project.html

38. https://quotepark.com/quotes/999326- nikola-tesla-if-you-want-to-find-the-secrets-of- the-universe-t/

39. Smarter Than You Think by Clive Thompson. William Collins Publishers, 2013.

40. Real Time with Bill Maher (HBO 24 Jan 2020)

41. "Choir singing improves health, happiness – and is the perfect icebreaker." The Conversation – Jacques Launay, Postdoctoral Researcher in Experimental Psychology, University of Oxford

42. https://www.nytimes.com/2020/02/11/arts/music/joseph-shabalala-dead.html

43. https://www.britannica.com/biography/Joseph-Shabalala

44. https://www.britannica.com/biography/Joseph-Shabalala

45. Enlightenment Now Steven Pinker "The Case For Reason, Science, Humanism, and Progress" Penguin Books Ltd

46. https://www.wondriumdaily.com/inventedcalculus-newton-leibniz/

47. https://philosophynow.org/issues/30/Leibniz_and_the_Leaves_Beyond_Identity#

48. https://trumpwhitehouse.archives.gov> remarks-preside... 29 Feb 2020

49. https://en.wikipedia.org/wiki/Red_pill_and_blue_pill

50. Steven Kotler: Mapping Cloud Nine: Neuroscience, Flow, and the Upper Possibility Space of Human Experience. Audio CD - Sounds True; Unabridged edition (November 5, 2019)

51. Nakamura and Csíkszentmihályi, 1990: Flow: the https://en.wikipedia.org/wiki/Flow_(psychology)psychology of optimal experience. New York: Harper & Row

52. https://en.wikipedia.org/wiki/Flow_(psychology)

53. Divine Providence does not entirely Exclude Evil from Things: Thomas Aquinas – *Summa contra Gentiles*, Book III, c. 71, translated by

James F. Anderson (Notre Dame – London: University of Notre Dame Press, 1995)

54. From Google's English dictionary, provided by Oxford Languages

55. Bill Gates: The next outbreak? We're not ready. TED 03 Apr 2015

56. Smarter Than You Think by Clive Thompson. William Collins Publishers, 2013.

57. The Daily Show with Trevor Noah; Real Time with Bill Maher.

58. https://donaldrobertson.name/2018/01/18/ what-do-the-stoic-virtues-mean/

59. Kevin Roache: Why Most People Are Wrong Most Of The Time https://vocal.media/motivation/why-most-people-are-wrong-most- of-the-time

60. Rupert Sheldrake: A New Science of Life: The Hypothesis of Formative Causation (Tarcher, 1981)

61. Roy Lichtenstein (ArtHaus – Art and Design Series) Produced by Chris Hunt.

62. The Demise of Kodak: Five Reasons By Kamal Munir Feb. 26, 2012 The Wall Street Journal

63. Monkeyworlds.com

64. Ted Talk, Tim Urban, 2016

65. Trevor Noah The Social Distancing Show interview with Ricky Gervais 13 May 2020

66. Vital Statistics in the United States, 1940- 1960: Diseases and Vaccination By Trung Nguyen, Robert D. Grove, Alice M. Hetzel, US Department of Health, Education, and Welfare.

67. https://www.journaldemontreal. com/2020/11/27/le-terrain-est-tout

68. https://www.goodreads.com/quotes/551027-yesterday-i-was-clever-so-i-wanted-to-change- the

69. http://paulsimonsongs.blogspot. com/2013/07/the-girl-for-me.html

70. https://www.forbes.com/sites/ arielshapiro/2021/04/30/inside-paul-simons- catalog-sale-at-250-million-its-one-of-musics- biggest-bob-dylan/

71. http://paulsimonsongs.blogspot.com/p/blog-page.html

72. Invisible Wealth Arnold Kling and Nick Schultz Encounter Books (September 6, 2011)

73. Rumi Quotes & Poems | The Most Complete Selection of ... https://www.rumi.net › rumi_poems_main

74. https://www.drucker.institute/thedx/joes- journal-on-creating-the-future/

75. https://www.drucker.institute/thedx/joes-journal-on-creating-the-future/

76. Humankind: A Hopeful History, Rutger Bregman Little, Brown and Company; June 2, 2020

77. The Times newspaper (10 May 2020)

78. Humankind: A Hopeful History: Book Review Amazon.com

79. http://dictionary.com

80. Dictionary.com

81. Nat King Cole, Nature Boy Songwriters: Eden Ahbez, Nature Boy lyrics © Sony/ATV Music Publishing LLC

82. https://omilacombe.ca/law-nature-creation-not-live-creatures/

83. https://www.news24.com/news24/john-steenhuisen-we-need-fewer-wishbones-and-more-backbones-20191110

84. https://en.wikipedia.org/wiki/Day_of_Affirmation_Address (Author also attended 4 June 2016 at the University of Cape Town)

85. https://www.jLlibrary.org/learn/about- jL/the-kennedy-family/robert-f-kennedy/ robert-f-kennedy-speeches/day-of- affirmation-address-university-of-capetown- capetown-south-africa-june-6-1966

86. https://www.usatoday.com/story/news/ politics/2020/07/18/rep-john-lewis- most-memorable-quotes-get-good- trouble/5464148002/

87. https://en.wikipedia.org/wiki/ Metcalfe%27s_law

88. The Daily Guardian. https:// thedailyguardian.com/spiritual-beings- having-a-human-experience/

89. https://www.youtube.com/ watch?v=VwhMkA1p4e8

90. https://twitter.com/neiltyson/ status/345551599382446081?lang=en

91. https://aeon.co/essays/einstein-v-newton- the-final-battle-during-a-total-eclipse

92. https://www.psitek.net/pages/PsiTek- you-11.html

93. https://en.wikipedia.org/wiki/Snell%27s_ law

94. https://www.scribd.com/book/530472785/ Kunene-and-the-King

95. https://www.newsweek.com/boseman- biden-kamala-harris-black-panther- tributes-1528522

96. Panther Chadwick Boseman's advice to new graduates. https://.bbc.com › news › newsbeat-4410835

www.ingramcontent.com/pod-product-compliance
Lightning Source LLC
Chambersburg PA
CBHW031512040426
42445CB00009B/198

9780796151261